W0391186

# The New York Times

## MINI CROSSWORDS:
## 150 Easy Fun-Sized Puzzles
## Volume 1

By Joel Fagliano

ST. MARTIN'S GRIFFIN NEW YORK

THE NEW YORK TIMES MINI CROSSWORDS VOLUME 1.

Printed in China. For information, address St. Martin's Press, 175 Fifth Avenue, New York, NY 10010.

www.stmartins.com



ISBN 978-1-250-14800-1



First Edition: October 2017

10 9 8 7 6 5 4

# The New York Times

## MINI CROSSWORDS

# The New York Times

## MINI CROSSWORDS

# Looking for more Easy Crosswords?

# The New York Times

## The #1 Name in Crosswords

Available at your local bookstore or online at nytimes.com/store/books

St. Martin's Griffin

# Introduction

When you think about it, crosswords are particularly well-suited for our fast-paced, modern age. Almost every clue and answer is on a different subject, your mind bounces from one thing to the next, and when a puzzle's not too hard, it takes only a short time to do.

Well, if regular crosswords are modern, *The New York Times*'s new Mini crosswords are hypermodern. The clues and answers are just as diverse, but each 5×5-square grid takes a mere minute or so to complete—even less once you get good. You now feel the rush of excitement in finishing a puzzle in a fraction of the time!

Launched in 2014, and originally available only digitally, the Mini has become so popular that now on weekdays it also appears in print in the main section of the paper.

Each Mini is created by Joel Fagliano, the paper's digital crosswords editor, who started selling regular crosswords to the *Times* when he was seventeen. To date he's had more than 50 weekday and Sunday crosswords published in the paper, becoming in the process one of the most popular and accomplished puzzlemakers.

Joel packs his Minis with lively vocabulary, modern references, and the sort of playfulness and intelligence you'll find in its big brother elsewhere in the paper. The Minis are easy/medium in difficulty. The cultural references skew young. But don't let the small size and big squares fool you. These puzzles are decidedly for adults.

On the following pages are 150 Minis from the *Times,* lightly re-edited for their first publication in book form.

Let the many rushes of excitement begin!

—Will Shortz

**ACROSS**

**1** "Downton Abbey" airer

**4** U.C.L.A. athlete

**6** Ruffles potato chip feature

**7** "You ____ to know better"

**8** Word with the longest entry in the O.E.D.

**DOWN**

**1** Car that's popular among progressives

**2** Barely move

**3** One of the senses

**4** Many a fraternity member, in modern slang

**5** Brooklyn baller

# 2

**ACROSS**

**1** Snapple flavor ___ Madness

**6** Caught sight of

**7** 5-Down + 7-Down

**8** Gets hitched

**9** Beginning

**DOWN**

**2** Looking like you've seen a ghost

**3** Willy Wonka candy

**4** V-formation fliers

**5** E's value, in Scrabble

**7** The only even prime number

# 3

**ACROSS**

**1** Final opponent, in video games
**5** Dusty room, typically
**7** "Take it easy, dude"
**8** Convention nametag word
**9** Take a breather

**DOWN**

**1** Composer described as "the original father of harmony"
**2** Last choice on a questionnaire, often
**3** Subway feature
**4** Places for houseplants
**6** Coagulate

# 4

**ACROSS**

**1** Choose (to)

**4** 2013 NBA champions

**6** NBA team where Shaq started his career

**8** Team that's made the NBA playoffs 29 times but never won the championship

**9** Letter before omega

**DOWN**

**1** Unit of electrical resistance

**2** Food items catapulted by a spoon, perhaps

**3** Get ready to run, in baseball

**5** Altoids containers

**7** CBS hit with two spin-offs

# 5

| | | | | |
|---|---|---|---|---|
| 1 | 2 | 3 | 4 | 5 |
| 6 | | | | |
| 7 | | | | |
| 8 | | | | |
| 9 | | | | |

**ACROSS**

**1** Eyeballs

**6** Love, to Luigi

**7** Fortuneteller's deck

**8** Believer in Karma

**9** Succumb to narcolepsy

**DOWN**

**1** "@&#^$%!" and such

**2** Microsoft Outlook competitor

**3** Michaels of "S.N.L."

**4** Chip away at

**5** Provide with a blind date

# 6

| | | | | |
|---|---|---|---|---|
| 1 | 2 | 3 | 4 | 5 |
| 6 | | | | |
| 7 | | | | |
| 8 | | | | |
| 9 | | | | |

**ACROSS**

**1** "The Expendables 3" co-star
**6** Truism
**7** Backs with bucks
**8** "Practice makes perfect," e.g.
**9** Button on the Wii console

**DOWN**

**1** "Aladdin" villain
**2** Give off
**3** Turner and Fey
**4** Mountain getaway
**5** "No more for me, thanks"

# 7

## ACROSS

**1** Rental car add-on

**4** L.L. Bean rival

**6** "Fingers crossed"

**7** Count in music

**8** Word with party or bag

## DOWN

**1** Popular IM service

**2** "You campaign in poetry. You govern in ___": Mario Cuomo

**3** Common Instagram filter

**4** Triangular sail

**5** Minute

# 8

**ACROSS**

**1** Recede, as the tide

**5** 2013 Rock and Roll Hall-of-Fame inductees

**7** Grammy-winning alt-rock band

**8** "Dancing Queen" group

**9** Pauses on sheet music

**DOWN**

**2** Under-the-table payment

**3** They're sold at hardware stores and garden shops

**4** "Tommy" group, with "The"

**6** Sing like Ella Fitzgerald

**7** "Low Rider" band

**ACROSS**

**1** Buddy

**5** Epic ___

**7** "Nuthin' But a 'G' Thang" rapper

**8** Acronym often said before doing something ill-advised

**9** You've reached it for the Across clues

**DOWN**

**2** Hairdo for Bill de Blasio's son

**3** Soup scoop

**4** The "A" of IPA

**6** Monopoly token that was recently replaced by a cat

**7** Add highlights to

# 10

| | | | | |
|---|---|---|---|---|
| 1 | ■ | 2 | 3 | |
| 4 | 5 | | | ■ |
| 6 | | | | 7 |
| ■ | 8 | | | |
| 9 | | | ■ | |

**ACROSS**

**2** Unruly head of hair
**4** Kind of speed, in "Star Trek"
**6** Pop duo with the 2011 #1 hit "Party Rock Anthem"
**8** Growth on old bread
**9** UPS Store purchase

**DOWN**

**1** Creature capable of 270-degree head rotation
**2** Dahl's "Fantastic" title character
**3** Gemstone for most Libras
**5** Firing range rounds
**7** Like all prime numbers but one

# 11

**ACROSS**

**1** ___ talks (annual idea conferences)

**4** Popular action figure

**6** Now and then preceder

**7** "Lost" character named after a philosopher

**8** Many a college dorm room, metaphorically

**DOWN**

**1** Saves for later viewing

**2** DVD player button

**3** Like a dweeb

**4** Shampoo or toothpaste, e.g.

**5** Optometrist's focus

# 12

**ACROSS**

**1** Dieter's meal, perhaps

**6** Had on

**7** "You never know"

**8** "Whatever you say, boss"

**9** Language from which corgi and crag come

**DOWN**

**2** Up

**3** Faithful

**4** Fast food chain known for its roast beef

**5** "Look at me, I'm Sandra ___" ("Grease" song)

**7** Tend to the lawn

**ACROSS**

**1** Precious stone
**5** Extinct bird
**7** White-feathered wader
**8** Freshwater duck
**9** Fail a polygraph test

**DOWN**

**2** Rim
**3** Lesson from Aesop
**4** Legalized substance in Colorado and Washington
**6** Where cold cuts are cut
**7** "Too many to list" abbr.

# 14

| | | | | |
|---|---|---|---|---|
| 1 | 2 | 3 | 4 | 5 |
| 6 | | | | |
| 7 | | | | |
| 8 | | | | |
| 9 | | | | |

**ACROSS**

**1** Intro to American Politics, e.g.

**6** ___-Loompa (Willy Wonka employee)

**7** Some sex shop purchases

**8** Scrabble pieces

**9** Run-down

**DOWN**

**1** Super Bowl winners in 2006

**2** FX show starring a red-headed comedian

**3** Mosey along

**4** Radar gun reading

**5** Impertinent

# 15

**ACROSS**

**1** Internet, with "the"
**5** Green shade
**7** Brown shade
**8** Yellow shade
**9** Mind reader's ability, briefly

**DOWN**

**2** Mr. Noodle's friend on "Sesame Street"
**3** Book in many a hotel room
**4** 2013 Spike Jonze movie
**6** Docs prescribe them
**7** Popular boot brand

## 16

### ACROSS

**2** Utility bill item

**4** Malicious computer program

**6** His Secret Service code name was Renegade

**8** Supply-and-demand subject, informally

**9** Watch closely

### DOWN

**1** Atomic number of helium

**2** Apt name for an elegant woman

**3** Bullets, e.g.

**5** Carry out, as orders

**7** Bug in "A Bug's Life"

# 17

**ACROSS**

**1** Poke fun at

**4** Annoy

**6** Work unit

**7** "Yeah, but even so"

**8** Place for a trough

**DOWN**

**1** Takes to the streets

**2** Words after "You can't fire me"

**3** Moe in "Calvin and Hobbes," e.g.

**4** Undercover outfit, briefly?

**5** Sushi bar order

# 18

**ACROSS**

**1** Curse

**4** Uncle on a poster

**5** Onetime capital of Japan that anagrams to the current capital

**7** "Glee" network

**8** Kim Kardashian, to Kanye

**DOWN**

**1** Leno of late-night

**2** "Gotta run!"

**3** Console for the game Halo

**4** Depict in a biased way

**6** Ballerina's pivot point

# 19

**ACROSS**

**1** Apple product
**4** Tripoli's country
**6** Burglary deterrent
**7** Hop out of bed
**8** Happy response to a marriage proposal

**DOWN**

**1** With 3-Down, MTV's Artist of the Year for 2013
**2** Lessen
**3** See 1-Down
**4** Fall behind
**5** Rock band equipment

## 20

### ACROSS

**2** Snapple product
**4** Corn Belt state
**6** Stylish, in slang
**8** Canadian tribe
**9** Himalayan beast

### DOWN

**1** Image file seen on many Tumblr pages
**2** Dance like Miley Cyrus at the VMA's
**3** Effortlessness
**5** SeaWorld sight
**7** Curse

# 21

## ACROSS

**1** Slightly open, as a door

**4** Go fish alternative

**6** "This is the worst!"

**8** Harry Potter's pet Hedwig, e.g.

**9** Mice, to cats

## DOWN

**1** Like about half of a team's games

**2** Prominent crocodile feature

**3** Knight's protection

**5** Right turn ___

**7** Wonderment

# 22

**ACROSS**

**1** Closest buddy, in textspeak

**4** Monte ___ (Vegas casino)

**6** Motorola smartphone

**7** Call on a computer

**8** Plea at sea

**DOWN**

**1** Hounds' sounds

**2** Alternative to soft serve, informally

**3** Somersaults

**4** Composition of many a music library

**5** Praiseful poem

# 23

**ACROSS**

**1** Part of L.A.

**4** Give a quick greeting

**6** Tylenol rival

**7** Salesperson

**8** CBS symbol

**DOWN**

**1** Soup-serving utensil

**2** Yiddish "Yikes!"

**3** Hobbit's homeland, with "The"

**4** ___ fly (certain baseball hit, for short)

**5** Sort

# 24

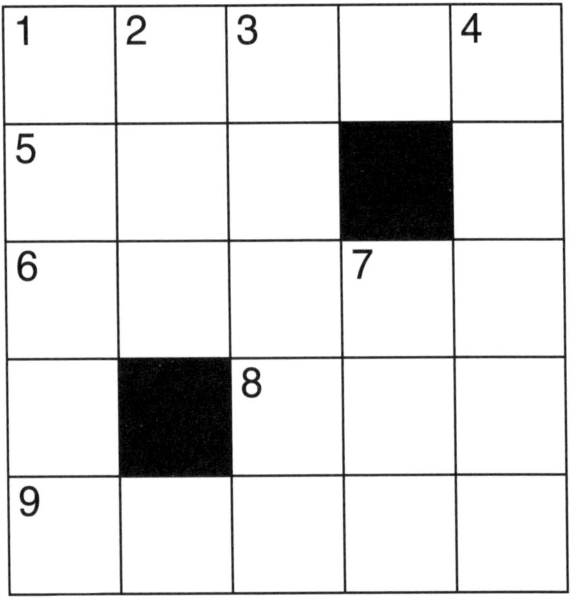


**ACROSS**

**1** Tavern offering
**5** The "p" in m.p.h.
**6** Tavern offering
**8** Tavern offering
**9** Armored vehicles

**DOWN**

**1** Hard-to-make spare
**2** Drink served with crumpets
**3** Heart or liver
**4** What the Michelin Man is made out of
**7** Antlered animal

# 25

## ACROSS

**1** What a violinist might have or take

**4** "Whoops, I goofed"

**6** "Don't ___," teacher's message in chalk to a janitor

**7** Frolics

**8** Yea's opposite

## DOWN

**1** Lord of poetry

**2** First president whose name ends in a vowel other than E or Y

**3** Stereotypically upper-crust

**4** Debussy's "La ___"

**5** ___ Moines, Iowa

# 26

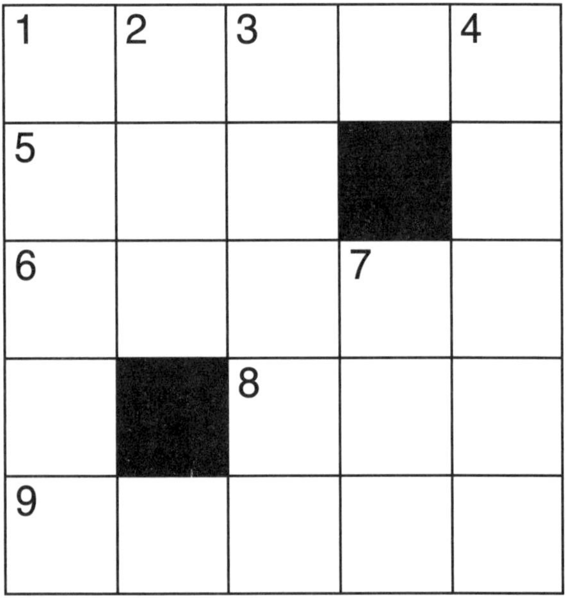

**ACROSS**

**1** Path down to a mine

**5** Prominent feature of an Obama caricature

**6** Smiley face with hearts for eyes, e.g.

**8** "Holy moly!"

**9** Last name of two presidents

**DOWN**

**1** "Peace!"

**2** Deli order

**3** Cinnabon lure

**4** Womb mates?

**7** Improvise, as a band

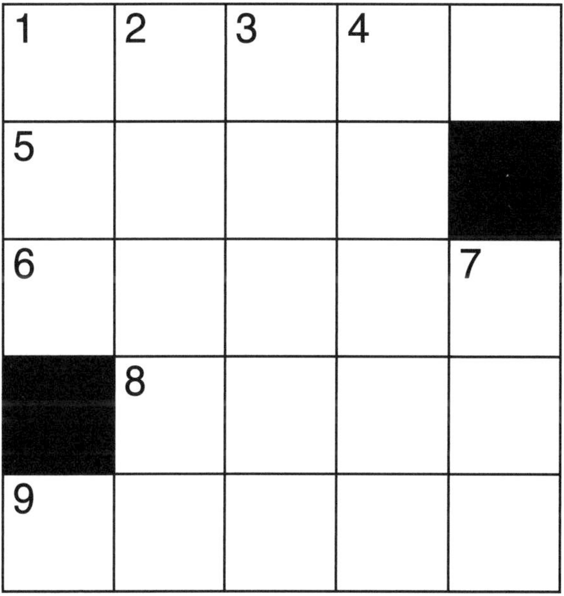

**ACROSS**

**1** Silly

**5** Bar Mitzvah, e.g.

**6** Order of the Phoenix member, in the Harry Potter books

**8** "Silver Linings Playbook" star, in tabloids

**9** 2008 Pixar movie about a robot

**DOWN**

**1** Receiver of many Apr. checks

**2** Assassin in black

**3** In the least

**4** Land with half of Mount Everest

**7** Fan of the rams?

# 28

**ACROSS**

**1** Sphere

**5** Black-and-white predator

**7** Rapper with the 2007 #1 "Buy U A Drank"

**8** Prefix with morphosis

**9** Animal house?

**DOWN**

**2** Tug-of-war requirement

**3** Brand of teenage dolls

**4** Homo sapiens

**6** "I'm outta here"

**7** Celebrity gossip website

# 29

| | | | | |
|---|---|---|---|---|
| 1 | 2 | 3 | 4 | 5 |
| 6 | | | | |
| 7 | | | | |
| 8 | | | | |
| 9 | | | | |

**ACROSS**

**1** Mosey along
**6** Big name in copiers
**7** Shake an Etch A Sketch
**8** Neighbor of the pancreas
**9** Video game controller button

**DOWN**

**1** Figure skating jumps
**2** ____ badge, Boy Scout award
**3** Cheer for an opera star
**4** Complete dweeb
**5** Put forth, as effort

# 30

| | | | | |
|---|---|---|---|---|
| 1 | ■ | 2 | 3 | 4 |
| 5 | 6 | | | |
| 7 | | | | |
| 8 | | | | |
| 9 | | | ■ | |

**ACROSS**

**2** Cut the grass

**5** Big appliance maker

**7** "Oh, for goodness ___!"

**8** Reward for a well-behaved dog

**9** Suffix with priest or lion

**DOWN**

**1** With 2- and 4-Down, adage about rushing

**2** See 1-Down

**3** Prime draft status

**4** See 1-Down

**6** Where the Curiosity rover is

**ACROSS**

**1** Place for many a modern-day rant

**5** Work very hard

**6** Piece of cake?

**7** Sky-blue

**8** Cried one's eyes out

**DOWN**

**1** What a firefighter fights

**2** Easy basketball shot

**3** In-your-face

**4** Richard of "Pretty Woman"

**5** Shredded side dish

## 32

**ACROSS**

**1** Red "Sesame Street" character

**4** Diving seabird

**6** Orange "Sesame Street" character

**8** Machine tooth

**9** Yellow "Sesame Street" character

**DOWN**

**1** Corp. higher-up

**2** Itchy canine ailment

**3** Parisian assent

**5** Retained

**7** Shoplift from

**ACROSS**

**1** Place for a mani-pedi
**4** Number below a You Tube video
**6** "There, there"
**7** Bad, informally
**8** Dessert with a crust

**DOWN**

**1** Abs strengthener
**2** Joe of "GoodFellas"
**3** Stopped sleeping
**4** Word on either side of "-à-"
**5** What's up?

# 34

**ACROSS**

**1** Puts two and two together

**5** Kansas City NFL player

**7** Philadelphia NFL player

**8** Buffalo NFL player

**9** Cleverness

**DOWN**

**1** Great tennis serve

**2** Abu ____

**3** Sudoku fill-in

**4** Place on eBay

**6** Pool table material

# 35

**ACROSS**

**1** #27 in a history sequence

**4** Beanie Babies or Angry Birds

**5** #44 in a history sequence

**7** Cat call

**8** Satellite signal receiver

**DOWN**

**1** Key above Caps Lock

**2** #2 in a history sequence

**3** Melting period

**4** #38 in a history sequence

**6** "I'm less than impressed"

# 36

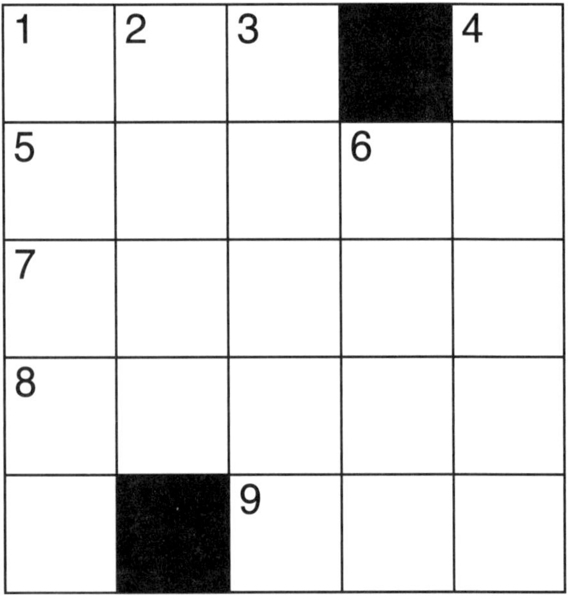


**ACROSS**

**1** Number of points for a safety, in football

**5** "Yippee!"

**7** Its license plates say "Famous potatoes"

**8** Listerine targets

**9** Hurricane's center

**DOWN**

**1** Campfire base

**2** Walk in the kiddie pool

**3** United hub

**4** Maine's state animal

**6** "Holy cow!"

# 37

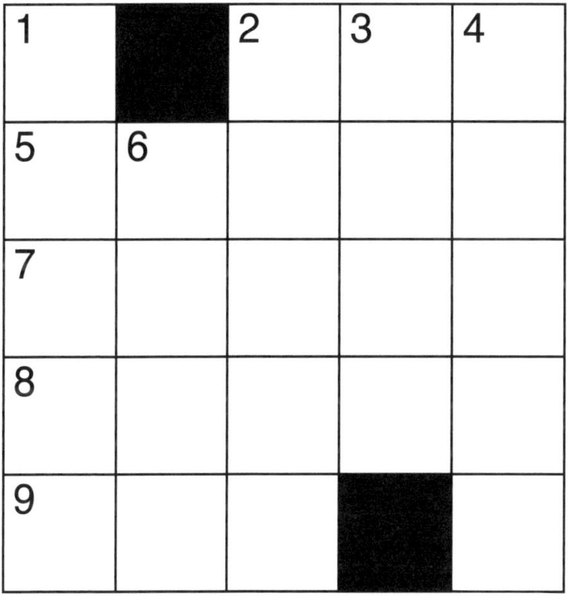

**ACROSS**

**2** Tank filler

**5** Admission of ineptitude

**7** Site of the 2014 Olympics

**8** Indiana basketballer

**9** Hit the slopes

**DOWN**

**1** Speaks like Daffy Duck

**2** Louis Vuitton competitor

**3** Feeling after a long run

**4** Word before steak or chaser

**6** Take a nice, long bath

# 38

| | | | | |
|---|---|---|---|---|
| ■ | 1 | 2 | 3 | ■ |
| 4 | | | | 5 |
| 6 | | | | |
| 7 | | | | |
| | ■ | 8 | | |

**ACROSS**

**1** White lie

**4** "Anaconda" rapper Nicki

**6** "Someone Like You" singer

**7** Singer with the 2013 #1 hit "Royals"

**8** Recipe amt.

**DOWN**

**1** Stereotypical dog's name

**2** Like radon and krypton

**3** Loses one's hair

**4** Chamber of commerce?

**5** Grand Cherokee maker

| | | | | |
|---|---|---|---|---|
| 1 | ■ | 2 | 3 | |
| 4 | 5 | | | ■ |
| 6 | | | | 7 |
| ■ | 8 | | | |
| 9 | | | ■ | |

**ACROSS**

**2** Paper ____ (annoying printer problem)

**4** Out-of-focus picture, e.g.

**6** Garment that's a portmanteau word

**8** Missing part of the Great Sphinx of Giza

**9** That woman

**DOWN**

**1** President after J.F.K.

**2** One of 12 at a trial

**3** Section of the Times where the crossword is found, with "The"

**5** Sole

**7** Reason for an R rating

# 40

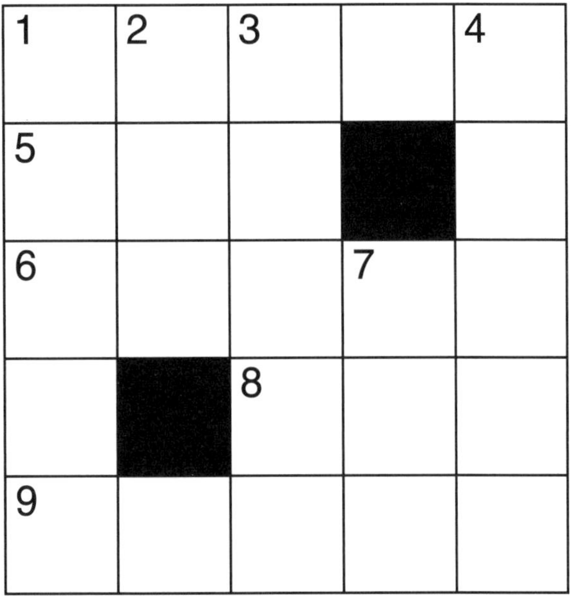


**ACROSS**

**1** Part of a table setting

**5** 2011 Huffington Post purchaser

**6** Part of a table setting

**8** Feb. follower

**9** Part of a table setting

**DOWN**

**1** Stares open-mouthed

**2** "Omg ur so funny!!!"

**3** "Remember the ___!"

**4** Back of a boat

**7** Eastern philosophy

| | | | | |
|---|---|---|---|---|
| 1 | 2 | 3 | 4 | 5 |
| 6 | | | | |
| 7 | | | | |
| 8 | | | | |
| 9 | | | | |

**ACROSS**

**1** Nixon's undoing in Watergate

**6** Up in the air

**7** Camera that may be attached to a ski helmet

**8** The "U" in E.U.

**9** Tubular pasta

**DOWN**

**1** What a runner may do during a fly ball

**2** Without a chaperon

**3** Show up unannounced

**4** Actor Zac of "Neighbors"

**5** Item in the sport of curling

# 42

**ACROSS**

**1** Toast topping
**5** Irish dances
**7** Sent electronically, in a way
**8** Plow pullers
**9** It sells, per an advertising adage

**DOWN**

**2** Sink-cleaning brand
**3** Some DJ creations
**4** "Lucy in the Sky With Diamonds" subject, supposedly
**6** Chromosome component
**7** Sly animal

## 43

| | | | | |
|---|---|---|---|---|
| 1 | 2 | 3 | 4 | 5 |
| 6 | | | | |
| 7 | | | | |
| 8 | | | | |
| 9 | | | | |

**ACROSS**

**1** Sidewalk artist's medium

**6** Bird in a Poe poem

**7** Lessen

**8** Viscous green material in Nickelodeon specials

**9** Black Friday events

**DOWN**

**1** Vulgar

**2** "Se ___ español"

**3** To no ___ (unsuccessfully)

**4** "Please, I'll take care of that"

**5** Joints with caps

# 44

| | | | | |
|---|---|---|---|---|
| | 1 | 2 | 3 | 4 |
| 5 | | | | |
| 6 | | | | |
| 7 | | | | |
| 8 | | | | |

**ACROSS**

**1** Stinging response to a crude pick-up line

**5** "Battlestar Galactica" genre

**6** World leader who was once a KGB officer

**7** Late film critic Roger

**8** "I double-dog ___ you!"

**DOWN**

**1** Swim with the fishes, say

**2** Soda bottle size

**3** Burning

**4** Blood donation unit

**5** Hurried

# 45

**ACROSS**

**1** "Game of Thrones" airer

**4** ___ trap (surprise warfare tactic)

**6** Change

**7** Makeup bag item

**8** Body spray that teenage boys tend to overuse

**DOWN**

**1** "Wassup!"

**2** Wrinkle-reducing shot

**3** Like "The Biggest Loser" contestants

**4** Word after sleeping, shopping or punching

**5** Soph. and jr.

## 46

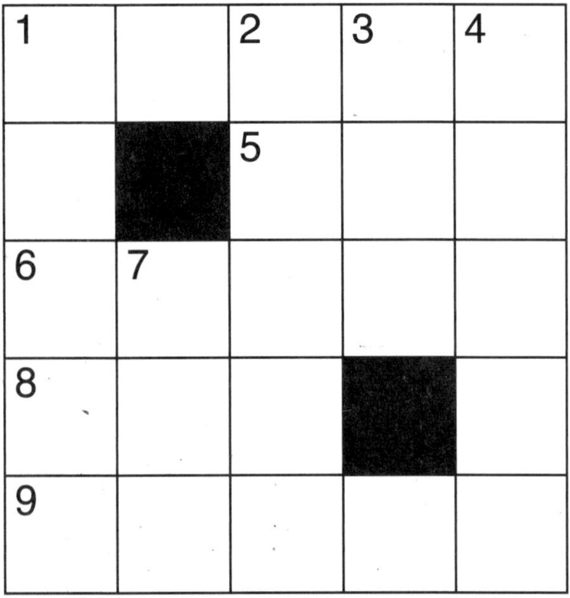


**ACROSS**

**1** One of life's certainties, per Benjamin Franklin

**5** Org. that makes bucks from the Bucks

**6** Variety of violet

**8** ___ Direction (U.K. boy band)

**9** One of life's certainties, per Benjamin Franklin

**DOWN**

**1** Bus station

**2** Take without permission, as territory

**3** Conan O'Brien's network

**4** U.S. president after Grant

**7** ___ Lucia Cortez ("Lost" character)

## ACROSS

**1** Enemy

**4** Dentist's directive

**6** Dentist's directive

**7** Muppet who lives in a trash can

**8** Item that's really annoying to lock in a car

## DOWN

**1** Stop and ____ (controversial police tactic)

**2** Maximum quantity of marijuana that it is legal to possess in Washington

**3** First section of the SAT, e.g.

**4** Muscular, party-loving dude, in modern parlance

**5** The Beatles' "I Saw ____ Standing There"

# 48

| | | | | |
|---|---|---|---|---|
| 1 | 2 | 3 | 4 | 5 |
| 6 | | | | |
| 7 | | | | |
| 8 | | | | |
| 9 | | | | |

**ACROSS**

**1** Language akin to Urdu

**6** With "The," source of the headline "Yahoo! Launches Soul-Search Engine"

**7** Neatniks' opposites

**8** Restaurant booth alternative

**9** "Awesome!"

**DOWN**

**1** Party throwers

**2** Oft-maligned family member

**3** Crier of Greek myth

**4** Paso ___ (Spanish dance)

**5** Magnified map detail

# 49

| | | | | |
|---|---|---|---|---|
| ■ | 1 | 2 | 3 | 4 |
| 5 | | | | |
| 6 | | | | |
| 7 | | | | |
| 8 | | | | ■ |

**ACROSS**

**1** Doodle Jump and Fruit Ninja
**5** Dance seen in Nicki Minaj's "Anaconda" video
**6** Capital of Vietnam
**7** Many Al Jazeera viewers
**8** Not doing anything

**DOWN**

**1** Employee-of-the-Month, e.g.
**2** Prison-related
**3** Exploratory spacecraft
**4** Sports equipment that's often waxed
**5** Cuisine with tom yum soup

# 50

**ACROSS**

**1** Mini

**4** Word between ready and fire

**5** Mini

**7** Something tossed up in the air after graduating

**8** Mini

**DOWN**

**1** Apple CEO Cook

**2** They might run Lion or Leopard

**3** Big name in crowd-sourced restaurant reviews

**4** Italian wine region

**6** ___ of the land

# 51

| | | | | |
|---|---|---|---|---|
| 1 | 2 | 3 | 4 | 5 |
| 6 | | | | |
| 7 | | | | |
| 8 | | | | |
| 9 | | | | |

## ACROSS

**1** Looks for

**6** Company that merged with Mobil in 1999

**7** "The Mysteries of ___" (2014 NBC debut)

**8** Respected tribe member

**9** The "turf" part of "surf and turf"

## DOWN

**1** Tennis champion with a palindromic name

**2** Praise mightily

**3** Radiate

**4** Where to get some Seoul food

**5** Sarcastic comments

# 52

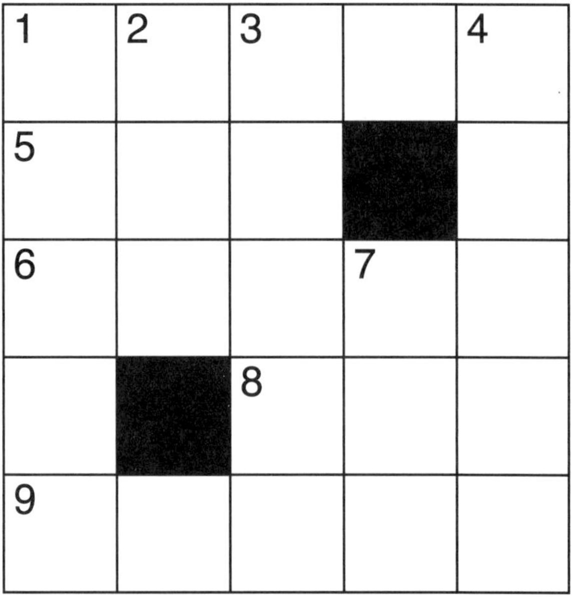


**ACROSS**

**1** Photo caption in a weight loss ad

**5** Wall Street index, with "the"

**6** Night vision?

**8** Internet ____ (our current time period)

**9** World leader reprimanded in Obama's 2014 U.N. speech

**DOWN**

**1** Make sense

**2** Part of FYI

**3** Alternative to a Facebook status

**4** Caesar or Brutus

**7** "Entourage" agent Gold

# 53

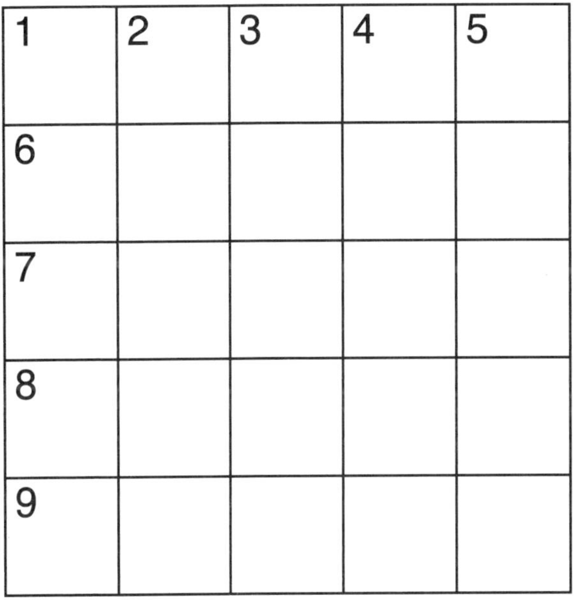


**ACROSS**

**1** "Relax, bro"

**6** Friend, in hip-hop lingo

**7** Not sleeping

**8** Tony the Frosted Flakes mascot, e.g.

**9** Run-down, as a motel

**DOWN**

**1** Uses WhatsApp or AIM

**2** "America's Got Talent" judge Mandel

**3** JPEG file, e.g.

**4** Showed one's appreciation for, as a Facebook status

**5** Distrustful

# 54

## ACROSS

**2** Pringles container

**5** Like 5-Across, vis-à-vis 7-Across

**7** Like 7-Across, vis-à-vis 5-Across

**8** Body parts that may be furrowed

**9** Red Roof ___

## DOWN

**1** Sermon giver on Rosh Hashanah

**2** Punctuation mark that makes emoticon eyes

**3** Declare

**4** Full of gossip

**6** Capital of Switzerland

# 55

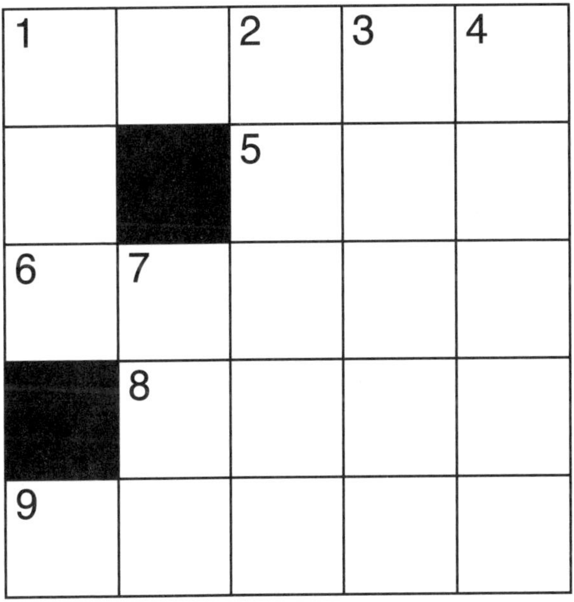


**ACROSS**

**1** "The Pine Tree State"
**5** One of three in the word Fiji
**6** Dumpster contents
**8** "The Buckeye State"
**9** ___ Light (pub choice)

**DOWN**

**1** Yoga class need
**2** "The Gem State"
**3** Boot camp reply
**4** Set of guiding beliefs
**7** Pal of Pooh

# 56

| | | | | |
|---|---|---|---|---|
| 1 | 2 | 3 | | 4 |
| 5 | | | ■ | |
| 6 | | | 7 | |
| | ■ | 8 | | |
| 9 | | | | |

**ACROSS**

**1** Eisenberg of "The Social Network"

**5** "Let's make ___ true Daily Double, Alex"

**6** Golden Arches pork sandwich

**8** Hubbub

**9** ". . . see what I mean?"

**DOWN**

**1** First name of two late-night hosts

**2** List-shortening abbr.

**3** Plastic wrap brand

**4** Funny bone's locale

**7** Words before "You may kiss the bride"

# 57

## ACROSS

**1** Bra part

**5** Jay Pharoah played him on S.N.L.

**7** Following the law

**8** Rapper with the 2013 #1 album "Nothing Was the Same"

**9** Ping-pong table divider

## DOWN

**1** Winter ailments

**2** App for getting a cab ride

**3** Polytheistic worshipper

**4** Person you may give your car keys to

**6** Manufacture

# 58

**ACROSS**

**1** Extra energy

**6** Greek goddess of marriage

**7** Greek god of the dead

**8** Greek god of war

**9** Make fun of

**DOWN**

**2** ORD, on an airline ticket

**3** Jason's wife in Greek myth

**4** ___ secretary (White House role)

**5** "I Can ___ Cheezburger?" (internet meme)

**7** Monopoly token choice

# 59

### ACROSS

**1** With 9-Across, show one's approval on the app Tinder

**5** Gear tooth

**6** Actress Blunt of "Edge of Tomorrow"

**8** Long, long time

**9** See 1-Across

### DOWN

**1** See-through

**2** Cupcake topper

**3** Many a "Meet the Press" guest

**4** Country on the Red Sea

**7** "Voulez-vous coucher avec ___?"

# 60

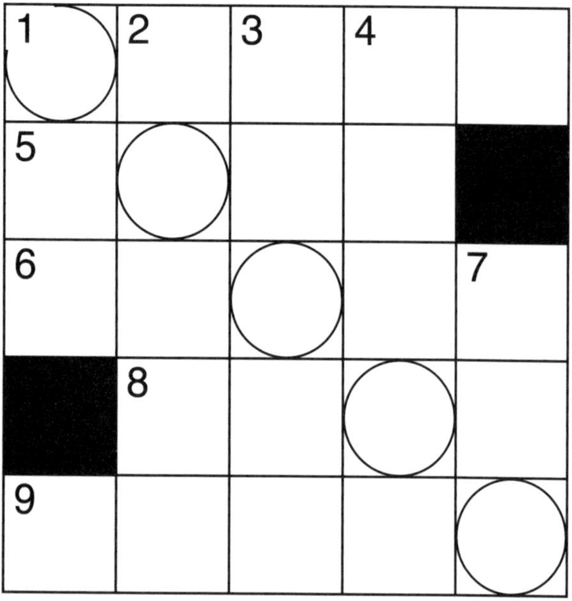


**ACROSS**

**1** Overly sentimental

**5** "Not guilty," e.g.

**6** Swing wildly

**8** Reason to use Clearasil

**9** Box for a pirate's treasure, maybe

**DOWN**

**1** Sunscreen letters

**2** God, in the Koran

**3** Nobel Prize category won by Malala Yousafzai

**4** "Growing ____" ('80s–90's sitcom)

**7** Tennis do-over

**ACROSS**

**1** Chess piece
**6** CAT scan alternative
**7** Chess piece
**9** Trendy boot brand
**10** Fictional captain who said "Thou damned whale!"

**DOWN**

**2** Last Greek letter
**3** Sought-after rock
**4** Chess piece
**5** Greenish-blue hue
**8** "This is the worst!"

# 62

| | | | | |
|---|---|---|---|---|
| 1 | 2 | 3 | 4 | 5 |
| 6 | | | | |
| 7 | | | | |
| 8 | | | | |
| 9 | | | | |

**ACROSS**

**1** Line of cliffs

**6** Studio that made "Up" and "Brave"

**7** Supreme Court justice Samuel

**8** Events that require bringing in the National Guard, maybe

**9** "Yeezus" rapper West

**DOWN**

**1** Romantic connection

**2** Scientific term for eyelashes

**3** Hypothetical physics particle

**4** Torn and tattered

**5** Nonpoetic writing

## ACROSS

**1** "Oops! I messed that up"

**5** Part of an airplane seat assignment

**6** Virus once screened for at JFK

**8** Stranded motorist's need

**9** Arabic : ibn :: English : ___

## DOWN

**1** Swimming competitions

**2** Ivy League school

**3** Gmail alternative

**4** One of a Disney septet

**7** Halloween sound

# 64

**ACROSS**

**1** Voter on a 2014 independence referendum

**5** New Zealand native

**6** Think alike

**7** Building blocks

**8** Target of current U.S. airstrikes

**DOWN**

**1** Wise ones

**2** Welsh ___ (dog breed)

**3** Snacks that are often deep-fried at carnivals

**4** Games nobody wins

**5** Burkina Faso neighbor

# 65

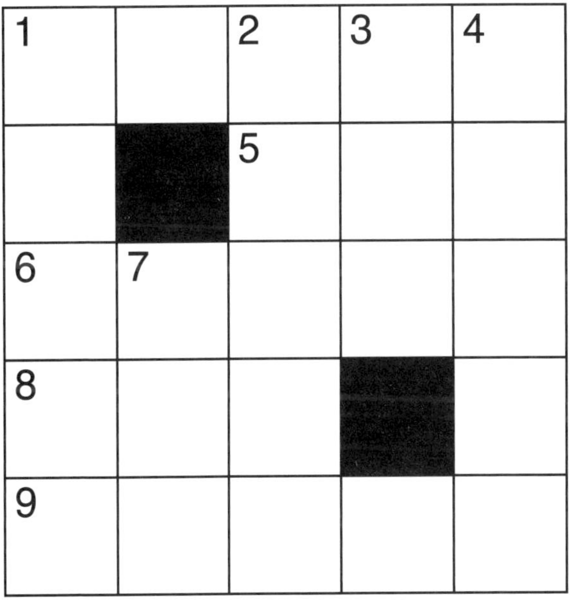


**ACROSS**

**1** With 1-Down, school troublemaker
**5** Illuminated
**6** Atmospheric layer
**8** Attempt to win over
**9** Like a party pooper

**DOWN**

**1** See 1-Across
**2** Standoffish
**3** "Everything that used to be a ___ is now a disease": Bill Maher
**4** Far from lenient
**7** Where the wild things are?

# 66

**ACROSS**

**1** Senses instinctively
**5** Christmas tree choice
**6** They're constantly tweeting
**8** Enemy
**9** Showed rage

**DOWN**

**2** Violin virtuoso Zimbalist
**3** Tupperware topper
**4** 12th graders: Abbr.
**6** Closest pal, briefly
**7** Debtor's letters

# 67

## ACROSS

**1** With 8-Across, stir-fried entrée

**4** "Monsters, Inc." girl

**5** Locked lavatory sign

**7** Drunkard

**8** See 1-Across

## DOWN

**1** Pro's opposite

**2** Electronic dance music genre

**3** Yeats or Keats

**4** Competes on eBay

**6** ___ milk (drink choice for a vegan)

# 68

**ACROSS**

**1** Cheerleader's boyfriend, say

**4** Drink with Flashin' Fruit Punch and Boppin' Strawberry flavors

**6** Intense media campaign

**8** Chris, to Peter, on "Family Guy"

**9** Place to hibernate

**DOWN**

**1** Perennial presidential campaign issue

**2** Country where dragon boat racing is popular

**3** Word after tool or shaving

**5** Ebola ____, 2014–15 White House position

**7** Gchat giggle

# 69

**ACROSS**

**1** Recently retired Yankee

**5** Designation for some batteries and minor-leaguers

**6** Clumsy sort

**8** Ages and ages

**9** Helicopter part

**DOWN**

**1** One of two in a deck of cards

**2** Talk smack to

**3** "____ my shorts!": Bart Simpson

**4** Cutting-edge technology?

**7** British bathroom

# 70

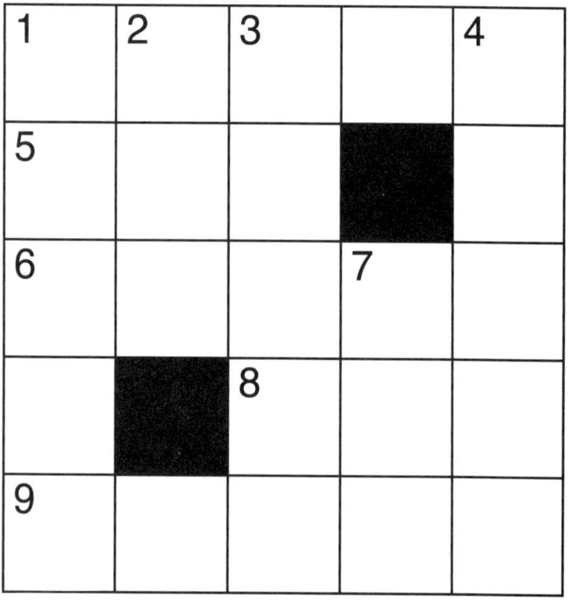


**ACROSS**

**1** 2014 World Series competitor

**5** Pitcher's pride

**6** Sully

**8** Drink with a string in it, perhaps

**9** 2014 World Series competitor

**DOWN**

**1** Swamp swimmer

**2** Glass of "This American Life"

**3** Cordial relations

**4** Completely wreck

**7** Teachers' lobbying org.

# 71

**ACROSS**

**1** Weather station's need

**6** Certain boozebag

**7** Standard graph axes

**8** Classic Jaguars

**9** Office supply store brand

**DOWN**

**2** Up and about

**3** Setting for some "Seinfeld" scenes

**4** "Then . . ."

**5** ___ Blount Jr., frequent "Wait Wait . . . Don't Tell Me!" panelist

**7** Bowler's turkey, on a scoresheet

# 72

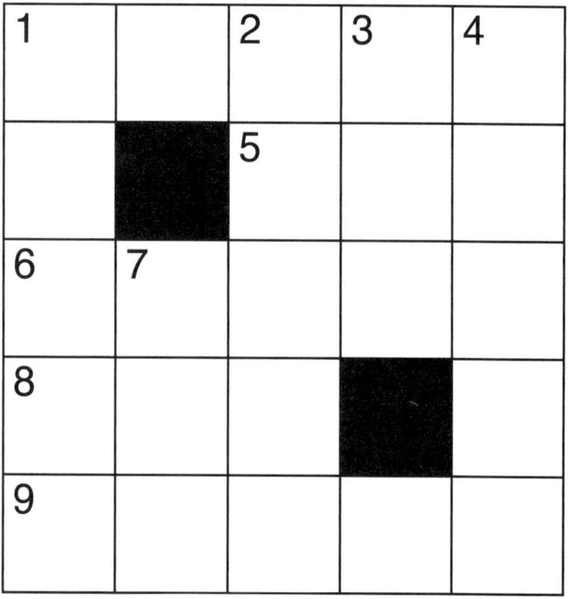


**ACROSS**

**1** Trick-or-treating accumulation

**5** All Hallow's ___ (another name for Halloween)

**6** "Gone With the Wind" protagonist Scarlett

**8** Crunchy Snickers bit

**9** Popular Halloween costume

**DOWN**

**1** Cheech's partner

**2** "Far out!"

**3** Not watch live, as a TV show

**4** Baker's supply

**7** "Whadja say?"

# 73

**ACROSS**

**1** Punched-out part of a paper ballot

**4** Setting for much of Homer's "Odyssey"

**5** Part of Congress

**7** Pecan or cashew

**8** Go to the polls

**DOWN**

**1** Dick Cheney vis-à-vis Halliburton, once

**2** Act like a ghost

**3** Weight Watchers offering

**4** Prisoner's knife

**6** Take to court

# 74

**ACROSS**

**1** Put two and two together?

**4** Bender

**6** With 7-Across, short story writer who won the 2013 Nobel Prize in Literature

**7** See 6-Across

**8** Difficult jigsaw puzzle area, maybe

**DOWN**

**1** Top grade

**2** Shirley Temple, for one

**3** Criticize sharply

**4** Cooke who sang "A Change is Gonna Come"

**5** Fair hiring letters

## ACROSS

**1** Spotify selection
**5** New York governor Andrew
**7** Being tried, as a case
**8** "I'm not even joking"
**9** Took a tumble

## DOWN

**1** Read, as a bar code
**2** "___ the Woods," lead single on Taylor Swift's "1989"
**3** Lord or lady
**4** Microsoft Outlook alternative
**6** ESPN sportscaster Hershiser

# 76

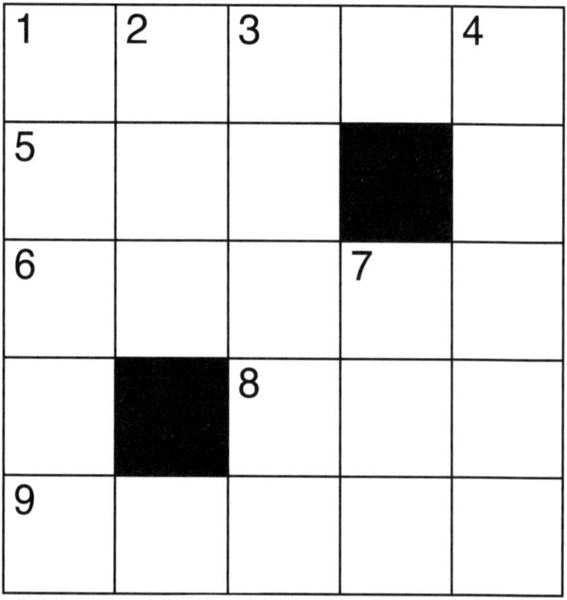


**ACROSS**

**1** Tylenol alternative

**5** ___ McGarry, chief of staff on "The West Wing"

**6** Tummy

**8** Golf bag item

**9** Ebenezer Scrooge, e.g.

**DOWN**

**1** ___ of the Year (Grammy category)

**2** Nearly failing grade

**3** Battery units

**4** Coat of paint

**7** Family name of about 15% of Koreans

# 77

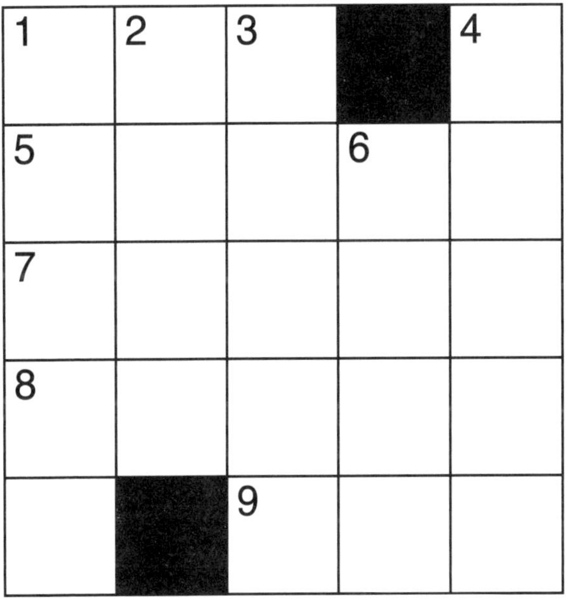

**ACROSS**

**1** President ___ tempore (Senate title)

**5** Make a director's version, say

**7** Senator McConnell

**8** Singer with the multiplatinum albums "19" and "21"

**9** Driveway material

**DOWN**

**1** Image shaper

**2** Former Senate Majority Leader Harry

**3** Days of Hanukkah, e.g.

**4** Common check box on surveys

**6** Home of the NCAA's Bruins

# 78

| | | | | |
|---|---|---|---|---|
| 1 | ■ | 2 | 3 | 4 |
| 5 | 6 | | | |
| 7 | | | | |
| 8 | | | | |
| 9 | | | ■ | |

**ACROSS**

**2** "Yo te ___" (Spanish "I love you")

**5** North America's only black billionaire

**7** Smoothie ingredient

**8** Penniless

**9** Wand-making material in "Harry Potter"

**DOWN**

**1** Destination of many a down elevator

**2** Certain computer key

**3** Grade, as papers

**4** "But of course!"

**6** Euro pop?

# 79

**ACROSS**

**1** x

**5** Whiz

**6** Happen

**8** Popular Vietnamese soup

**9** -

**DOWN**

**1** Time in Chicago when it's noon in L.A.

**2** City nicknamed "The Heart of Georgia"

**3** Old French coin

**4** Belgrade natives

**7** Energy, in feng shui

# 80

| | | | | |
|---|---|---|---|---|
| 1 | 2 | 3 | 4 | 5 |
| 6 | | | | |
| 7 | | | | |
| 8 | | | | |
| 9 | | | | |

**ACROSS**

**1** Off

**6** Double ___ (schoolyard game)

**7** Inflame

**8** Wrinkled fruit

**9** Messed (with)

**DOWN**

**1** Go with the flow

**2** British writer H.H. ___

**3** One to consult for PC problems

**4** Public spat

**5** Rip to pieces

# 81

**ACROSS**

**1** Places with feeding times
**5** SportsCenter segment
**6** Not just big-boned
**7** Challah part
**8** Without

**DOWN**

**1** What Marty is, in the movie "Madagascar"
**2** Continental divide?
**3** Band with the 1995 hit "Wonderwall"
**4** Went over the limit
**5** Sticks up

# 82

**ACROSS**

**1** Disney's Herbie, for one

**5** "Come hungry. Leave happy" chain

**6** Sister of Kate Middleton

**8** Like the score at the start of the 10th inning

**9** One way to get around D.C.

**DOWN**

**1** Kind of pass that might get you backstage

**2** One side in chess

**3** Hasbro toy with audio commands

**4** Word before hand or class

**7** Hubbub

# 83

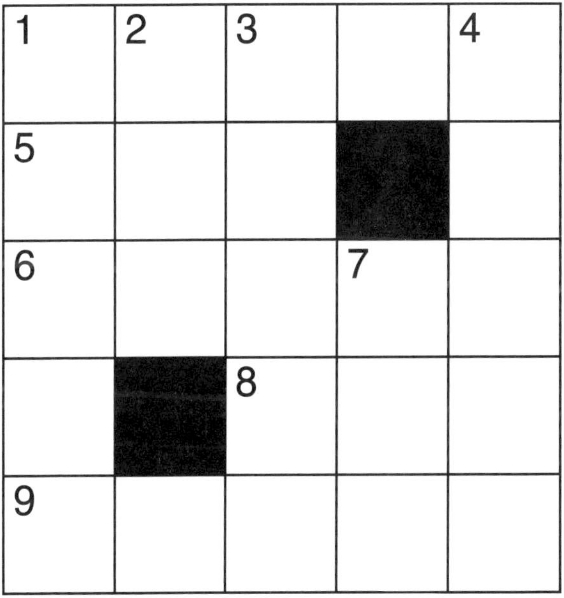

**ACROSS**

**1** Playground fixture
**5** Persona ___ grata
**6** Health insurance giant
**8** Owns
**9** Makes level

**DOWN**

**1** With 3- and 4-Down, treacherous person
**2** Distressed state
**3** See 1-Down
**4** See 1-Down
**7** Palindromic girl's name

# 84

| | | | | |
|---|---|---|---|---|
| 1 | 2 | 3 | 4 | 5 |
| 6 | | | | |
| 7 | | | | |
| 8 | | | | |
| 9 | | | | |

**ACROSS**

**1** Post office device

**6** Wrote in Python, say

**7** Together (with)

**8** Teenager who won the 2014 Grammy for Song of the Year

**9** Garlic ___

**DOWN**

**1** Place for a rug

**2** Use a crayon

**3** Love, love, love

**4** Gives temporarily

**5** Pieces jigsaw puzzlers usually start with

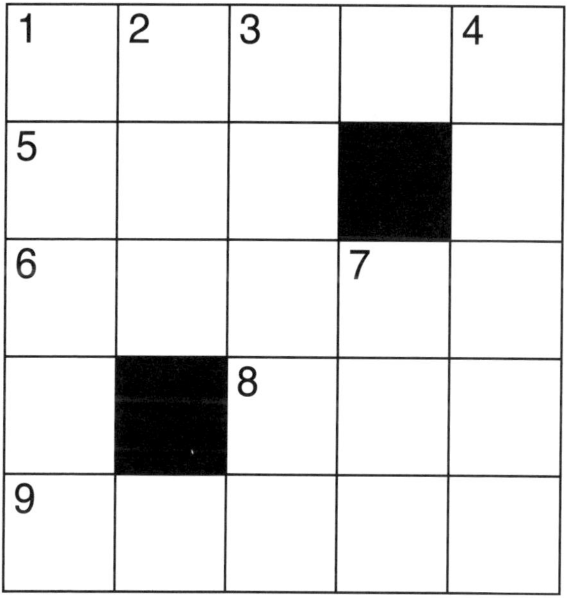

**ACROSS**

**1** Friend of Fozzie Bear

**5** Blue ___ Carter, Jay-Z and Beyoncé's kid

**6** Rank for Tom in Bowie's "Space Oddity"

**8** Flock female

**9** "Revolutionary Road" novelist Richard

**DOWN**

**1** Hobbling around, say

**2** Lab eggs

**3** Geno Smith or Michael Vick, once

**4** Shrek and Fiona

**7** Have bills to pay

# 86

| | | | | |
|---|---|---|---|---|
| 1 | ■ | 2 | 3 | 4 |
| 5 | 6 | | | |
| 7 | | | | |
| 8 | | | | |
| 9 | | | ■ | |

**ACROSS**

**2** Fix, as an election

**5** Wear away

**7** ____ diet (trendy nutritional plan)

**8** What a bald tire lacks

**9** Curse

**DOWN**

**1** Pool measurement

**2** Oft-counterfeited watch

**3** It might be half-baked

**4** Crystal-filled rock

**6** Like a white Bengal tiger

| | | | | |
|---|---|---|---|---|
| 1 | 2 | 3 | 4 | 5 |
| ■ | 6 | | | |
| 7 | | | | |
| 8 | | | | ■ |
| 9 | | | | |

**ACROSS**

**1** Astronaut's work environment, for short

**6** Like orange oranges

**7** Order that might come with schmear

**8** One needing tech support

**9** Airport annoyance

**DOWN**

**2** Clear, as a chalkboard

**3** Brightest star in Orion

**4** The Barber of Seville, e.g.

**5** Many a hand sanitizer

**7** Slang term for marijuana

# 88

**ACROSS**

**1** Heart chart: Abbr.

**4** "I agree"

**5** "I agree"

**6** "I agree"

**7** Take home the gold

**DOWN**

**1** Consumed

**2** "Gimme a break!"

**3** Prefix with politics or chemistry

**4** 18-wheeler

**5** Big mouth

# 89

**ACROSS**

**1** Like an eager guest, maybe
**5** Confederate uniform color
**6** Pull out all the stops
**8** Greedy person's cry
**9** Something earned after defeating a Gym Leader, in the Pokémon games

**DOWN**

**1** Item graded AA, A or B
**2** Fragrance
**3** Fanatical
**4** Saying "I won't laugh, I promise," usually
**7** "Well, I'll be darned!"

# 90

## ACROSS

**1** Email folder

**5** "This is so exciting!"

**7** Controversial 2013 Johnny Depp role

**8** 11th anniversary gift

**9** Roughly

## DOWN

**1** Drunks

**2** Instagram post, e.g.

**3** "Li'l" comics boy

**4** Dust particles

**6** Modern acronym said before doing something ill-advised, maybe

## ACROSS

**2** Subject line starter on many an e-mail joke
**5** Just the slightest bit
**7** Like Seattle, meteorologically
**8** Over-the-top Spanish accent?
**9** Golf champion Ernie

## DOWN

**1** À la ___ (one way to order)
**2** "Epic" mistakes, in modern lingo
**3** Weather vane turner
**4** Alternative to a clothesline
**6** Nasty winter weather

# 92

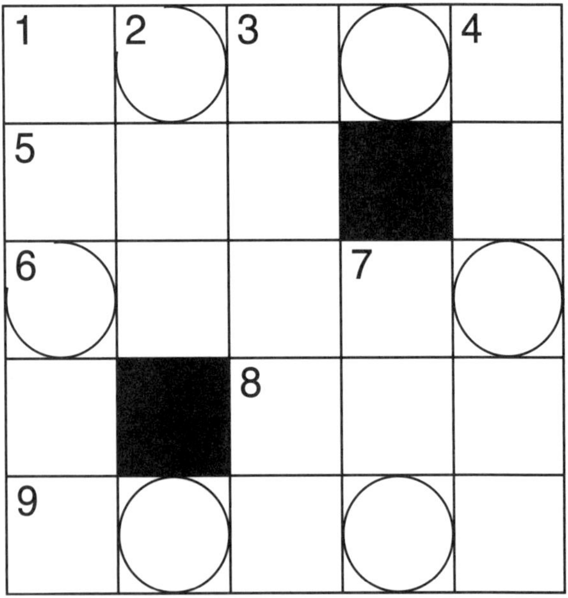


**ACROSS**

**1** Strong and pungent, as an odor

**5** Where the 2014 World Cup final was played

**6** Raring to go

**8** Fair ___ (copyright issue)

**9** Smart guy?

**DOWN**

**1** Madison Square Garden, e.g.

**2** Org. whose annual budget is classified

**3** Renegade

**4** Jeter called "Captain Clutch"

**7** Computer key

# 93

## ACROSS

**1** Alternative to a text
**5** Emotionally detached
**7** Klingon forehead feature
**8** Disney World has a Loch Ness monster made of them
**9** Fit inside one another, as Russian dolls

## DOWN

**1** Co-worker of Homer on "The Simpsons"
**2** 1979 sci-fi blockbuster
**3** Ski resort building
**4** Shell's shell and Apple's apple, e.g.
**6** Coachella or Lollapalooza, informally

# 94

| | | | | |
|---|---|---|---|---|
| 1 | 2 | 3 | 4 | 5 |
| 6 | | | | |
| 7 | | | | |
| 8 | | | | |
| 9 | | | | |

**ACROSS**

**1** Chess declaration

**6** Macho guy

**7** Ridiculous

**8** "It was ____ that changed angels into devils": St. Augustine

**9** Farm towers

**DOWN**

**1** Poker player's stack

**2** French painter Matisse

**3** Something checked on a smartphone, maybe

**4** Confident kind of attitude

**5** Strike zone's lower boundary

# 95

| | | | | |
|---|---|---|---|---|
| 1 | | 2 | 3 | 4 |
| | ■ | 5 | | |
| 6 | 7 | | | |
| 8 | | | ■ | |
| 9 | | | | |

**ACROSS**

**1** Scatterbrained

**5** Outdoor recreation gear chain

**6** One way to get home for Thanksgiving

**8** ___ chi (martial art)

**9** Sharpened, as skills

**DOWN**

**1** Complexity

**2** One way to get home for Thanksgiving

**3** ___ Master, nickname for coaching legend Phil Jackson

**4** Triangular road sign

**7** Neighbor of a Thai

96

**ACROSS**

**1** Thanksgiving season

**4** Deli order

**5** One-up

**7** McKellen who played Gandalf

**8** Thanksgiving parade sponsor

**DOWN**

**1** Winter woe

**2** Room at the top?

**3** N.F.L. team that hosts a game every Thanksgiving

**4** Rapid economic expansion

**6** Turkey ___ (Thanksgiving nickname)

# 97

## ACROSS

**1** Item on a chairlift

**4** Barbera's partner in animation

**6** "Dude (Looks Like ___)" (Aerosmith song)

**7** Carl who was chairman of the Senate Armed Services Committee

**8** SpongeBob's home

## DOWN

**1** Black Friday events

**2** Rapscallion

**3** Country that recently elected Narendra Modi Prime Minister

**4** "Shallow" guy in a 2001 rom-com

**5** Novelist Rand

# 98

**ACROSS**

**1** Member of an Iraqi minority

**4** Stephen's partner on Comedy Central

**5** Food that Mayor de Blasio controversially ate with a fork

**7** Na+, e.g.

**8** Stare in wonder

**DOWN**

**1** Fancy pond swimmer

**2** Open, as a jacket

**3** Vernon Wormer in "Animal House," e.g.

**4** Image file format

**6** Actress Saldana of "Guardians of the Galaxy"

**ACROSS**

**2** Theater ticket specification

**4** Flat

**6** War on ____ (catchphrase used in reproductive rights debates)

**8** Facebook button

**9** "____ is the most fun you can have without laughing": Woody Allen

**DOWN**

**1** Captain Kirk or Harrison Ford, per Sandler's "The Chanukah Song"

**2** DJ's creation

**3** Short race distance, briefly

**5** Mouselike animal

**7** Just out of the package

# 100

**ACROSS**

**1** LeBron James's team, informally

**5** Student

**6** First president with a Twitter account

**7** Longtime "Whose Line Is It Anyway?" host

**8** Hold ___ (keep)

**DOWN**

**1** Fidel Castro, e.g.

**2** In pieces

**3** Youtube competitor

**4** Kill, as a dragon

**5** Somewhat, in music

# 101

**ACROSS**

**2** Number of pool pockets

**4** It's less than seven, in this puzzle's theme

**6** It's seven, in this puzzle's theme

**8** It's greater than seven, in this puzzle's theme

**9** ___ rent, sign outside a house

**DOWN**

**1** Something a dog "shakes hands" with

**2** George Harrison played one on "Norwegian Wood"

**3** Mid-March date

**5** Popular spring break destination, slangily

**7** Like strawberries and ketchup

# 102

| | | | | |
|---|---|---|---|---|
| 1 | 2 | 3 | 4 | 5 |
| 6 | | | | |
| 7 | | | | |
| 8 | | | | |
| 9 | | | | |

**ACROSS**

**1** N.J. city that was involved in the Bridgegate scandal

**6** Winner of four gold medals at the Berlin Olympics

**7** Uses a Kindle, say

**8** Italian birthplace of Columbus

**9** Contest submission

**DOWN**

**1** Fabricate, as a signature

**2** Many a Hunger Games fan

**3** Tilted

**4** Forested moon in "Return of the Jedi"

**5** Think piece, e.g.

# 103

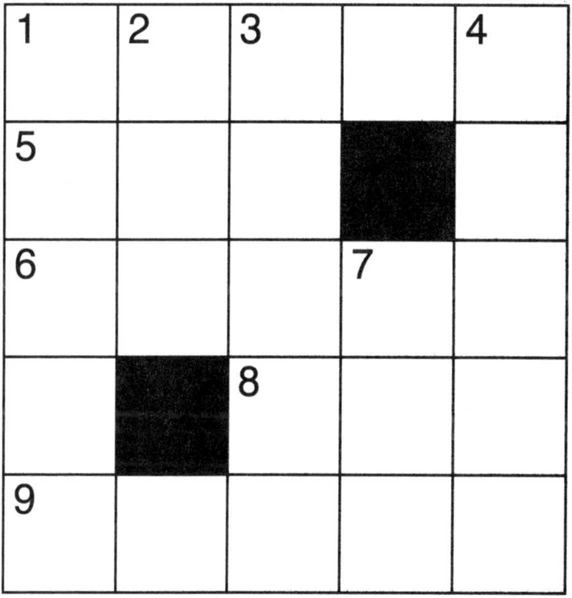


**ACROSS**

**1** U.S. city nicknamed the Big Guava

**5** Game console with a remote

**6** U.S. city whose name Peyton Manning used as an audible

**8** Deface

**9** U.S. city that hosts the Famous Idaho Potato Bowl

**DOWN**

**1** 32 oz.

**2** Point, as a pistol

**3** U.S. city with a large Cuban population

**4** Cognizant

**7** "___ the whole world gone mad?!"

# 104

**ACROSS**

**1** Bar mitzvah figure

**6** Audacity

**7** Chuck who was defense secretary from 2013–15

**8** Colored part of the eye

**9** Array in a man's closet, maybe

**DOWN**

**2** Plant from which tequila is made

**3** Breakfast order with a hole in it

**4** Sheep's cry

**5** "___ be back!" ("The Terminator" catchphrase)

**7** Philadelphia International Airport for American Airlines, e.g.

# 105

**ACROSS**

**1** Comedian Margaret

**4** Best Picture of 2005

**6** Its slogan begins "15 minutes could save you . . ."

**7** It may dangle from a dog collar

**8** Title for Mick Jagger or Alec Guinness

**DOWN**

**1** Photo ____ (Instagrammer's recognitions)

**2** Neighbor of the Dominican Republic

**3** Best Picture, e.g.

**4** Big budget item for a Michael Bay movie, probably

**5** Harley-Davidson, slangily

# 106

**ACROSS**

**1** ___ a fool (be ridiculous, in slang)

**5** "The Simpsons" character

**7** "The Simpsons" character

**8** Natural process that Hydra jellyfish don't undergo

**9** Prez before J.F.K.

**DOWN**

**2** What paper towels do to a toilet

**3** Not at all brave

**4** "The Simpsons" character

**6** Shoot off, as a text message

**7** Signature apparel for Pharrell

# 107

**ACROSS**

**1** "The Boy Who Cried Wolf" storyteller

**6** Message from the boss

**7** Amped up on caffeine

**8** Talk show guest's blatant promotion

**9** "Way to go, dude!"

**DOWN**

**2** Actress Deschanel of "Bones"

**3** Truth ___ (interrogation injection)

**4** Last Greek letter

**5** Modern prefix with cast

**7** Typist's stat.

# 108

| | | | | |
|---|---|---|---|---|
| ■ | 1 | 2 | 3 | 4 |
| 5 | | | | |
| 6 | | | | |
| 7 | | | | |
| 8 | | | | ■ |

**ACROSS**

**1** Many a Reddit post

**5** Smoked delicacies

**6** Put forth, as effort

**7** Pagan nature religion

**8** Post-monologue spot for Jimmy Fallon

**DOWN**

**1** Audacity

**2** Higher-ups, informally

**3** Pharmaceutical giant

**4** "Cómo ____?"

**5** Smutty

# 109

**ACROSS**

**1** "Kapow!"

**4** "Maleficent" star

**6** Winery process

**7** Florida senator Marco

**8** Certain family member, informally

**DOWN**

**1** Fake

**2** Something examined in a cross-examination

**3** Certain M&Ms

**4** Peanut butter purchase

**5** Self-image

# 110

## ACROSS

**1** Wine barrel

**5** ____ Bruni, wife of Nicolas Sarkozy

**6** 70 miles per hour, on many interstates

**7** What the bumper sticker "Your in America, speak English" exhibits

**8** Much-criticized Congressional spending

## DOWN

**1** Capital of Egypt

**2** Medieval museum exhibit

**3** Move stealthily

**4** Pop star Perry

**5** Part of many a Daily Show segment

**ACROSS**

**1** Does terribly, as a comedian

**6** Place to do laps

**7** Secretary of State from 2013–16

**8** Country with a Supreme Leader

**9** All 44 presidents, e.g.

**DOWN**

**2** "Madame Butterfly", e.g.

**3** Fable's lesson

**4** Carried

**5** Cunning

**7** North Korea's ___ Jong-un

# 112

| | | | | |
|---|---|---|---|---|
| ■ | 1 | 2 | 3 | 4 |
| 5 | | | | |
| 6 | | | | |
| 7 | | | | |
| 8 | | | | ■ |

**ACROSS**

**1** Journalistic no-no

**5** "Me too"

**6** ___ Sans, oft-ridiculed font

**7** Afghani's neighbor to the north

**8** Hot ___ (complete disaster, in slang)

**DOWN**

**1** Alcohol

**2** Patterns of stressed syllables, in poetry

**3** French friends

**4** "Totally rad, bro!"

**5** Pond layer

**ACROSS**

**1** Naughty

**4** Philosopher whose name is also a delicious breakfast food

**6** Japanese truck maker

**7** Parisian cap

**8** Dapper ___

**DOWN**

**1** "___ on a true story"

**2** Japanese luxury auto

**3** Krispy Kreme purchase

**4** Lobster eater's protection

**5** Bit of trail mix

## 114

**ACROSS**

**1** "___ birthday!"

**6** "Whatever you say"

**7** Rock of "Top Five"

**8** Bunch of buffalo

**9** English county or a Vermont town

**DOWN**

**2** Campfire remains

**3** Contented cat sounds

**4** One of the seven deadly sins

**5** "Of course!"

**7** Cohort of Fidel Castro

# 115

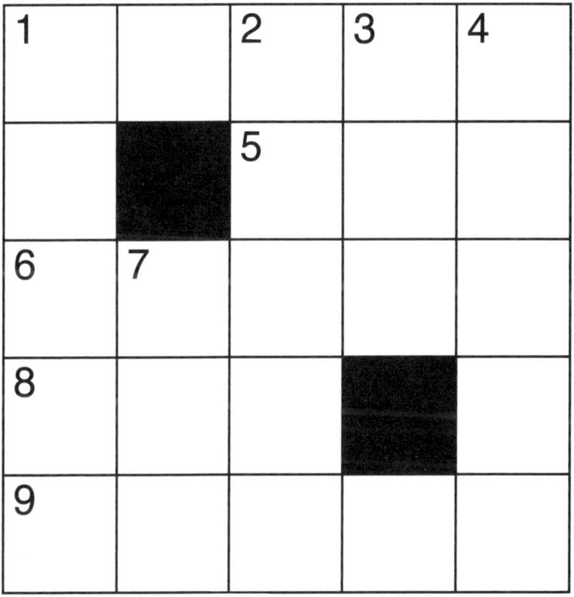

**ACROSS**

**1** Adorable one
**5** ____-com (movie genre)
**6** Profound difference in opinion
**8** Eco-friendly lightbulb
**9** Board meeting attendees, informally

**DOWN**

**1** The seasons or the phases of the moon, e.g.
**2** Commerce
**3** What Apple's mobile/tablet devices run on
**4** Awards show hosted in 2014 by Seth Meyers
**7** Bad spell

# 116

**ACROSS**

**1** "President Obama, John Boehner and a duck walk into ___ . . ."

**5** Subway feature

**6** "For real"

**7** Words that can be added to the end of any fortune cookie, it's said

**8** Menial worker

**DOWN**

**1** Make amends

**2** "The Hobbit" hero

**3** Illegal ___

**4** Part of a saxophone

**5** Sound at a barber shop

# 117

**ACROSS**

**1** Cunning

**5** Nickname for the South

**6** Sleep problem

**7** "This ___ war!"

**8** "Slow Churned" ice cream brand

**DOWN**

**1** Completely exhausted, slangily

**2** Pig Latin negative

**3** Property claims

**4** Thumbs-up votes

**5** Knight's wife

# 118

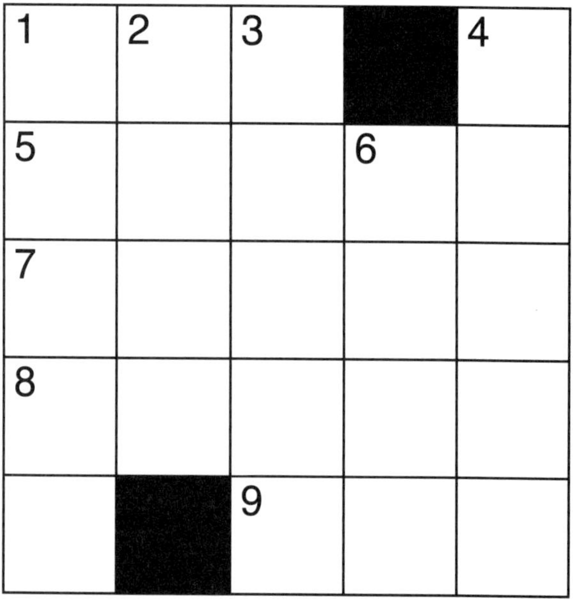


**ACROSS**

**1** Pickle holder

**5** Call to mind

**7** "Blurred Lines" singer Thicke

**8** Public, as information

**9** Windsor knot neckwear

**DOWN**

**1** Jack Link's product

**2** Stratford-upon-____

**3** Bender from "Futurama" or Rosie from "The Jetsons"

**4** Tube-shaped pasta

**6** Fuzzy fruit

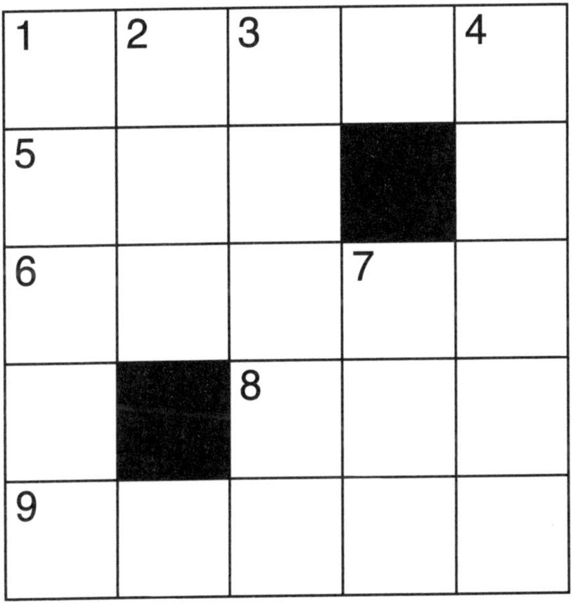


**ACROSS**

**1** Hanukkah snack

**5** Reaction to watching a baby animal video, maybe

**6** Duane ___ (pharmacy chain)

**8** Whoopi Goldberg in "Sister Act," e.g.

**9** Number of nights of Hanukkah

**DOWN**

**1** The "L" in XXL

**2** Wonder

**3** Country singer's sound

**4** Facebook invitation with a calendar icon

**7** "Thanks, Captain Obvious"

# 120

**ACROSS**

**1** "Yo"

**4** Wayne ___ (Batman's home)

**6** The "A" of A/V

**7** Without stopping

**8** Class with nude models

**DOWN**

**1** Spa feature

**2** ___ the mistletoe

**3** Use one's index finger, maybe

**4** Leader who said "Political power grows out of the barrel of a gun"

**5** Fishing pole

**ACROSS**

**1** Six-pack units

**5** Dog in the comic strip "Beetle Bailey"

**7** Dog in the comic strip "Hägar the Horrible"

**8** Dog in the comic strip "Garfield"

**9** Mint-condition

**DOWN**

**2** Dr. No foe

**3** Oktoberfest container

**4** Building site

**6** Christmas ___

**7** Ingredient in some lattes

# 122

| | | | | |
|---|---|---|---|---|
| 1 | 2 | 3 | 4 | 5 |
| 6 | | | | |
| 7 | | | | |
| 8 | | | | |
| 9 | | | | |

**ACROSS**

**1** ____ pants (multipocketed wear)

**6** Dream interrupter

**7** No longer following orders

**8** Victoria's Secret purchase

**9** Secret ____ (holiday activity)

**DOWN**

**1** Things seen at supermarkets or golf courses

**2** Hawaii hello

**3** Tease

**4** Weight room sound

**5** Watch brand that's also a Greek letter

## ACROSS

**1** Videotape type

**4** Spike Jonze's "___ John Malkovich"

**6** One way to sing

**7** Second-string squad

**8** Annoy

## DOWN

**1** 20-ounce Starbucks order

**2** One wearing a fanny pack and eating gorp, say

**3** ___ preview

**4** Baby's mealtime garment

**5** Average Joe's in "Dodgeball," e.g.

# 124

**ACROSS**

**1** It may start "I do solemnly swear . . ."

**4** "To each ___ own"

**6** Give a red card to

**8** Macklemore & Ryan Lewis, e.g.

**9** Bernie Madoff's hedge fund, for one

**DOWN**

**1** Piece by Gail Collins or Paul Krugman

**2** Fox series whose theme song was "California"

**3** Drunk's sound

**5** Flower's support

**7** Au ___ (how a French dip is served)

# 125

| | | | | |
|---|---|---|---|---|
| 1 | 2 | 3 | 4 | 5 |
| 6 | | | | |
| 7 | | | | |
| 8 | | | | |
| 9 | | | | |

**ACROSS**

**1** Sound from a smoke detector or cricket
**6** Send for a second opinion
**7** Boredom
**8** Teatime pastry
**9** French heads

**DOWN**

**1** Wave's high point
**2** Therefore
**3** "Otherwise . . ."
**4** Get together with old friends
**5** Opens someone else's emails, maybe

# 126

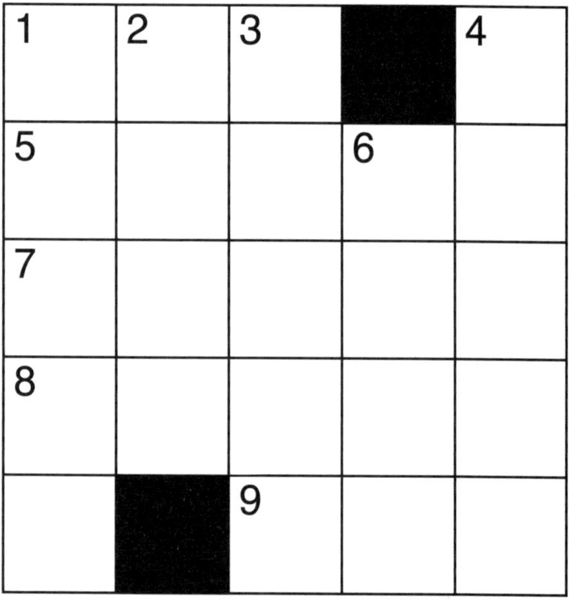

**ACROSS**

**1** Yukon S.U.V. maker

**5** Swiss mathematician who introduced "e" for natural logs

**7** Santa ___

**8** Butterfingers

**9** "That's what I was trying to tell you!"

**DOWN**

**1** Animal with sticky foot pads

**2** Ponder

**3** Santa ___

**4** Eat like a cow

**6** Art Deco icon

# 127

**ACROSS**

**1** Ink ____: octopus defense

**4** Celebrity chef Deen

**6** Not in a bottle, at a bar

**7** Dark beer

**8** Animal in a nativity scene

**DOWN**

**1** With 3-Down, role for Tim Allen, Ed Asner and Leslie Nielsen

**2** Lincoln and Ford, but not Clinton

**3** See 1-Down

**4** Opposite of neg.

**5** Spot-on

# 128

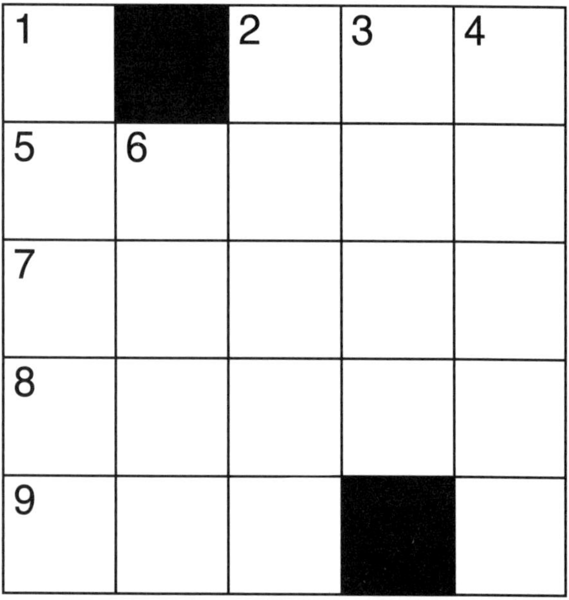


**ACROSS**

**2** Move like a bunny

**5** Remove a five-o'clock shadow, say

**7** Locale of a 2014 space landing

**8** Into pieces

**9** Hi-___ image

**DOWN**

**1** George Bluth Sr.'s identical brother on "Arrested Development"

**2** Gaza Strip governors

**3** "___ my dead body!"

**4** Of little importance

**6** ___ Diamond, display at the Smithsonian National History Museum

# 129

**ACROSS**

**1** Poetry contest

**4** Vessel for making lo mein

**6** Disney elephant

**8** "___ side note . . ."

**9** Egyptian symbol of life

**DOWN**

**1** Drink that carries an added tax in Berkeley, CA

**2** "This stinks!"

**3** Flash ___ (event coordinated through social media)

**5** Big name in conservative activism

**7** NAFTA signer

# 130

**ACROSS**

**1** Country the U.S recently re-established diplomatic relations with

**5** Onetime leader of 1-Across

**6** Rapper who co-founded Death Row Records

**7** They put the frosting on the cake

**8** Grant of old Hollywood

**DOWN**

**1** About, date-wise

**2** Milking-machine attachment

**3** Fruit in a tart

**4** Many microbrews

**5** Org. that enforces much of the Dodd-Frank Act

# 131

**ACROSS**

**1** 2015, in Roman numerals

**4** "Spare" thing at a barbecue

**6** Heart beater in bridge bidding

**8** Delivery from Santa

**9** Channel for armchair athletes

**DOWN**

**1** Event not to be missed

**2** Pictures at a hospital

**3** Posting on Vine, informally

**5** Peg with a baseball

**7** "The Premature Burial" author

# 132

**ACROSS**

**1** Alternative to brisket or sirloin

**5** ___ Bowl, sporting event on January 1st, 2015

**6** "We are ___" (2013 Song of the Year Grammy winner)

**8** Detest

**9** Kind of alarm or arrest

**DOWN**

**1** Weep

**2** Hullabaloo

**3** Par for the course

**4** What ".99" may represent

**7** "Well, whaddaya know!"

# 133

**ACROSS**

**1** With 8- and 9-Across, traditional New Year's song

**4** Sphere

**6** Chevy S.U.V. named for a lake

**8** See 1-Across

**9** See 1-Across

**DOWN**

**1** "A Bug's Life" bug

**2** "Mean Girls" star

**3** "Obama Spends Afternoon in Garage Restoring Classic ___" ("The Onion" headline)

**5** Plead

**7** 2012 Olympic gymnastics gold medalist ___ Raisman

# 134

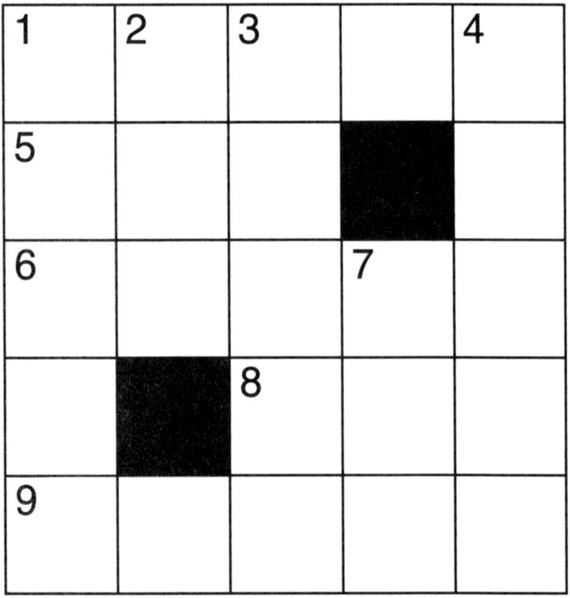

**ACROSS**

**1** Cowboy's rope

**5** Feel sick

**6** A ___ Called Quest (pioneering hip-hop duo)

**8** Member of New York's Finest, e.g.

**9** Eric B. and ___ (pioneering hip-hop duo)

**DOWN**

**1** "See ya!"

**2** Put on TV

**3** ___ Rick (early hip-hop icon)

**4** Hour after noon

**7** Big ___ (Outkast rapper)

# 135

**ACROSS**

**2** Austin Powers, e.g.

**4** First ____ (naval officer)

**6** Second-____ (question after the fact)

**8** Third-____(low-quality)

**9** Animal that symbolizes Aries

**DOWN**

**1** "That's, like, totally ridiculous"

**2** Teakettle emission

**3** Annoyance

**5** Mysterious glow

**7** Use needle and thread

# 136

**ACROSS**

**1** Washington chopping down the cherry tree, e.g.

**4** X : kiss :: O : ___

**6** Part of a driver's license

**8** Title at the Round Table

**9** Warm and cozy

**DOWN**

**1** Google ___

**2** Rosebush hazard

**3** "Survivor" shelter

**5** Instrument struck with a padded hammer

**7** Casual greetings

# 137

## ACROSS

**1** "Ya think?!"

**5** Cause of the witch's demise in "Hansel and Gretel"

**6** Frenzied

**8** Pussy ___ (Russian girl group)

**9** Songs from a choir

## DOWN

**1** When tripled, sound from a happy eater

**2** One end of a fallopian tube

**3** Jeans material

**4** The "U" of A.C.L.U.

**7** Dollar parts: Abbr.

# 138

**ACROSS**

**1** Real jerk
**4** Genre for B.B. King or Muddy Waters
**6** Martini garnish
**7** Big name in pads
**8** Japanese money

**DOWN**

**1** Bronze, but not silver or gold
**2** Honeymoon ___ (posh hotel offering)
**3** Atomic number of nitrogen
**4** ___ choy (Chinese vegetable)
**5** Cause for a TV-MA rating

# 139

| | | | | |
|---|---|---|---|---|
| 1 | 2 | 3 | 4 | ■ |
| 5 | | | | 6 |
| 7 | | | | |
| 8 | | | | |
| ■ | 9 | | | |

**ACROSS**

**1** Microsoft Office component

**5** Construction ___ (orange road sign)

**7** "Rise and ___!"

**8** Small coins for Brits

**9** Belgian river that was a W.W. I battle line

**DOWN**

**1** Stinging insect

**2** "Funny running into you here!"

**3** Jockey's handful

**4** The Dougie or The Stanky Leg

**6** Bucks and does

# 140

| | | | | |
|---|---|---|---|---|
| ■ | 1 | 2 | | 3 |
| 4 | | | ■ | |
| 5 | | | 6 | |
| | ■ | 7 | | |
| 8 | | | | ■ |

**ACROSS**

**1** Soft French cheese

**4** "___ you for real?"

**5** Mild Dutch cheese

**7** Dim ___ (Chinese food option)

**8** Like much wine and cheese

**DOWN**

**1** One wearing a lacrosse tank top, say

**2** Part of an environmental mantra

**3** Cheese in a red wheel

**4** Water, to Juan

**6** Firecracker that fizzles

# 141

| | | | | |
|---|---|---|---|---|
| 1 | 2 | 3 | ■ | 4 |
| ■ | 5 | | 6 | |
| 7 | | | | |
| 8 | | | | ■ |
| | ■ | 9 | | |

**ACROSS**

**1** Pokémon protagonist ___ Ketchum

**5** Jon of "Mad Men"

**7** One of the Seven Dwarfs

**8** "I'm such a klutz"

**9** "That's great news!"

**DOWN**

**2** "Go on, git!"

**3** One of the Seven Dwarfs

**4** Schumer of Comedy Central

**6** Mini-plateau

**7** One of the Seven Dwarfs

## 142

**ACROSS**

**1** "August: Osage County" or "Doubt"

**4** Little drink

**6** Horny beast?

**8** Calvin in "Calvin and Hobbes," e.g.

**9** "Lol, ur the best," for example

**DOWN**

**1** "The other white meat"

**2** Remark between actor and audience

**3** Yang's opposite

**5** Blog entry

**7** Google result

# 143

| | | | | |
|---|---|---|---|---|
| 1 | 2 | 3 | 4 | 5 |
| 6 | | | | |
| 7 | | | | |
| 8 | | | | |
| 9 | | | | |

**ACROSS**

**1** Toys used on snow days
**6** Video game stage
**7** Quick on one's feet
**8** German's "please"
**9** Porterhouse or T-bone

**DOWN**

**1** Thick slices
**2** Too ___ to quit (awesome, in slang)
**3** Something to RSVP to with a click
**4** Airline with a triangle logo
**5** Stylishly streamlined

# 144

**ACROSS**

**1** Kanye's wife
**4** Celebrate boisterously
**6** ___ Gay (W.W. II plane)
**7** Heat-resistant glassware
**8** "Sure thing, matey"

**DOWN**

**1** Birthplace of Obama's father
**2** Piano key material, once
**3** Super Smash Bros. ___ (popular video game)
**4** Dem.'s opponent
**5** Busiest airport on the West Coast, informally

# 145

**ACROSS**

**1** Filled with wonder
**5** Pixar film with a female protagonist
**6** Wranglers alternative
**7** Sweater style
**8** Nerf gun ammo

**DOWN**

**1** Madison Square Garden, e.g.
**2** Go back and forth in deciding
**3** Kick out
**4** ___ jockey: unhappy office worker
**5** Hollywood or Sunset: Abbr.

# 146

**ACROSS**

**1** Make bigger, as a bra

**4** Historical figure born on January 15, 1929

**6** Prize money

**7** Like hot fudge

**8** Explosive stuff

**DOWN**

**1** Hybrid fruit that's also called an apriplum

**2** Ohio city where LeBron James was born

**3** Gig for an aspiring electronica musician

**4** Car ad abbr.

**5** Spanish king

# 147

| | | | | |
|---|---|---|---|---|
| 1 | 2 | 3 | 4 | 5 |
| 6 | | | | |
| 7 | | | | |
| 8 | | | | |
| 9 | | | | |

**ACROSS**

**1** Blu-rays and frisbees

**6** Self-mover's rental

**7** Person-to-person payment app

**8** Really enjoy something, with "up"

**9** The "T" of L.G.B.T, informally

**DOWN**

**1** Bed cover

**2** "Word on the street is . . ."

**3** ___ Monica, California

**4** Spice often added to curries

**5** Vegas casino lineup

# 148

| | | | | |
|---|---|---|---|---|
| ■ | 1 | 2 | 3 | 4 |
| 5 | | | | |
| 6 | | | | |
| 7 | | | | |
| 8 | | | | ■ |

**ACROSS**

**1** Online source for TV shows
**5** Bouncing off the walls
**6** It helps you claim a suitcase
**7** Fumble around in the dark
**8** ____ Christian Andersen

**DOWN**

**1** Nine-headed serpent
**2** Supermodel Kate
**3** Tries to get a rebound
**4** Sexual desire, with "the"
**5** "____ five!" ("Borat" catchphrase)

# 149

**ACROSS**

**1** Covers with a cold blanket?

**6** 2014 movie based on a Broadway musical

**7** Hunky-dory

**8** Navy V.I.P.

**9** "Dee-licious!"

**DOWN**

**1** Impertinent

**2** Opposite of SSE

**3** When "S.N.L." ends in N.Y.C.

**4** 2014 movie starring Reese Witherspoon

**5** 2014 movie about Martin Luther King

# 150

**ACROSS**

**1** Christian Bale's role in 2014's "Exodus: Gods and Kings"

**4** Fruit that comes in a bunch

**7** Fruit often cut into balls

**8** Fruit that can be candied

**DOWN**

**1** Molten volcanic rock

**2** Resell, as sports tickets

**3** A great actor might steal one

**5** Ride for, in rap slang

**6** D.C. insider

# ANSWERS

**1**

| | | | | |
|---|---|---|---|---|
| | P | B | S | |
| B | R | U | I | N |
| R | I | D | G | E |
| O | U | G | H | T |
| | S | E | T | |

**2**

| | | | | |
|---|---|---|---|---|
| M | A | N | G | O |
| | S | E | E | N |
| T | H | R | E | E |
| W | E | D | S | |
| O | N | S | E | T |

**3**

| | | | | |
|---|---|---|---|---|
| B | O | S | S | |
| A | T | T | I | C |
| C | H | I | L | L |
| H | E | L | L | O |
| | R | E | S | T |

**4**

| | | | | |
|---|---|---|---|---|
| O | P | T | | |
| H | E | A | T | |
| M | A | G | I | C |
| | S | U | N | S |
| | | P | S | I |

**5**

| | | | | |
|---|---|---|---|---|
| O | G | L | E | S |
| A | M | O | R | E |
| T | A | R | O | T |
| H | I | N | D | U |
| S | L | E | E | P |

**6**

| | | | | |
|---|---|---|---|---|
| J | E | T | L | I |
| A | X | I | O | M |
| F | U | N | D | S |
| A | D | A | G | E |
| R | E | S | E | T |

## 7

| | | | | |
|---|---|---|---|---|
| | G | P | S | |
| J | C | R | E | W |
| I | H | O | P | E |
| B | A | S | I | E |
| | T | E | A | |

## 8

| | | | | |
|---|---|---|---|---|
| E | B | B | | W |
| | R | U | S | H |
| W | I | L | C | O |
| A | B | B | A | |
| R | E | S | T | S |

## 9

| | | | | |
|---|---|---|---|---|
| P | A | L | | A |
| | F | A | I | L |
| D | R | D | R | E |
| Y | O | L | O | |
| E | | E | N | D |

## 10

| | | | | |
|---|---|---|---|---|
| O | | M | O | P |
| W | A | R | P | |
| L | M | F | A | O |
| | M | O | L | D |
| B | O | X | | D |

## 11

| | | | | |
|---|---|---|---|---|
| | T | E | D | |
| G | I | J | O | E |
| E | V | E | R | Y |
| L | O | C | K | E |
| | S | T | Y | |

## 12

| | | | | |
|---|---|---|---|---|
| S | A | L | A | D |
| | W | O | R | E |
| M | A | Y | B | E |
| O | K | A | Y | |
| W | E | L | S | H |

## 13

| | | | | |
|---|---|---|---|---|
| G | E | M | | P |
| | D | O | D | O |
| E | G | R | E | T |
| T | E | A | L | |
| C | | L | I | E |

## 14

| | | | | |
|---|---|---|---|---|
| C | L | A | S | S |
| O | O | M | P | A |
| L | U | B | E | S |
| T | I | L | E | S |
| S | E | E | D | Y |

## 15

| | | | | |
|---|---|---|---|---|
| W | E | B | | H |
| | L | I | M | E |
| U | M | B | E | R |
| G | O | L | D | |
| G | | E | S | P |

## 16

| | | | | |
|---|---|---|---|---|
| T | | G | A | S |
| W | O | R | M | |
| O | B | A | M | A |
| | E | C | O | N |
| E | Y | E | | T |

## 17

| | | | | |
|---|---|---|---|---|
| | R | I | B | |
| P | I | Q | U | E |
| J | O | U | L | E |
| S | T | I | L | L |
| | S | T | Y | |

## 18

| | | | | |
|---|---|---|---|---|
| | J | I | N | X |
| S | A | M | | B |
| K | Y | O | T | O |
| E | | F | O | X |
| W | I | F | E | |

## 19

| | | | | |
|---|---|---|---|---|
| | M | A | C | |
| L | I | B | Y | A |
| A | L | A | R | M |
| G | E | T | U | P |
| | Y | E | S | |

## 20

| | | | | |
|---|---|---|---|---|
| G | | T | E | A |
| I | O | W | A | |
| F | R | E | S | H |
| | C | R | E | E |
| Y | A | K | | X |

## 21

| | | | | |
|---|---|---|---|---|
| A | J | A | R | |
| W | A | R | | O |
| A | W | M | A | N |
| Y | | O | W | L |
| | P | R | E | Y |

## 22

| | | | | |
|---|---|---|---|---|
| | B | F | F | |
| C | A | R | L | O |
| D | R | O | I | D |
| S | K | Y | P | E |
| | S | O | S | |

## 23

| | | | | |
|---|---|---|---|---|
| | L | O | S | |
| S | A | Y | H | I |
| A | D | V | I | L |
| C | L | E | R | K |
| | E | Y | E | |

## 24

| | | | | |
|---|---|---|---|---|
| S | T | O | U | T |
| P | E | R | | I |
| L | A | G | E | R |
| I | | A | L | E |
| T | A | N | K | S |

## 25

| | | | | |
|---|---|---|---|---|
| | B | O | W | |
| M | Y | B | A | D |
| E | R | A | S | E |
| R | O | M | P | S |
| | N | A | Y | |

## 26

| | | | | |
|---|---|---|---|---|
| S | H | A | F | T |
| E | A | R | | W |
| E | M | O | J | I |
| Y | | M | A | N |
| A | D | A | M | S |

## 27

| | | | | |
|---|---|---|---|---|
| I | N | A | N | E |
| R | I | T | E | |
| S | N | A | P | E |
| | J | L | A | W |
| W | A | L | L | E |

## 28

| | | | | |
|---|---|---|---|---|
| O | R | B | | M |
| | O | R | C | A |
| T | P | A | I | N |
| M | E | T | A | |
| Z | | Z | O | O |

## 29

| | | | | |
|---|---|---|---|---|
| A | M | B | L | E |
| X | E | R | O | X |
| E | R | A | S | E |
| L | I | V | E | R |
| S | T | A | R | T |

## 30

| | | | | |
|---|---|---|---|---|
| H | | M | O | W |
| A | M | A | N | A |
| S | A | K | E | S |
| T | R | E | A | T |
| E | S | S | | E |

## 31

| | | | | |
|---|---|---|---|---|
| ■ | B | L | O | G |
| S | L | A | V | E |
| L | A | Y | E | R |
| A | Z | U | R | E |
| W | E | P | T | ■ |

## 32

| | | | | |
|---|---|---|---|---|
| E | L | M | O | ■ |
| X | ■ | A | U | K |
| E | R | N | I | E |
| C | O | G | ■ | P |
| ■ | B | E | R | T |

## 33

| | | | | |
|---|---|---|---|---|
| ■ | S | P | A | ■ |
| V | I | E | W | S |
| I | T | S | O | K |
| S | U | C | K | Y |
| ■ | P | I | E | ■ |

**34**

| | | | | |
|---|---|---|---|---|
| A | D | D | S | ■ |
| C | H | I | E | F |
| E | A | G | L | E |
| ■ | B | I | L | L |
| W | I | T | ■ | T |

**35**

| | | | | |
|---|---|---|---|---|
| ■ | T | A | F | T |
| F | A | D | ■ | H |
| O | B | A | M | A |
| R | ■ | M | E | W |
| D | I | S | H | ■ |

**36**

| | | | | |
|---|---|---|---|---|
| T | W | O | ■ | M |
| W | A | H | O | O |
| I | D | A | H | O |
| G | E | R | M | S |
| S | ■ | E | Y | E |

## 37

| | | | | |
|---|---|---|---|---|
| L | ■ | G | A | S |
| I | S | U | C | K |
| S | O | C | H | I |
| P | A | C | E | R |
| S | K | I | ■ | T |

## 38

| | | | | |
|---|---|---|---|---|
| ■ | F | I | B | ■ |
| M | I | N | A | J |
| A | D | E | L | E |
| L | O | R | D | E |
| L | ■ | T | S | P |

## 39

| | | | | |
|---|---|---|---|---|
| L | ■ | J | A | M |
| B | L | U | R | ■ |
| J | O | R | T | S |
| ■ | N | O | S | E |
| H | E | R | ■ | X |

**40**

| | | | | |
|---|---|---|---|---|
| G | L | A | S | S |
| A | O | L | | T |
| P | L | A | T | E |
| E | | M | A | R |
| S | P | O | O | N |

**41**

| | | | | |
|---|---|---|---|---|
| T | A | P | E | S |
| A | L | O | F | T |
| G | O | P | R | O |
| U | N | I | O | N |
| P | E | N | N | E |

**42**

| | | | | |
|---|---|---|---|---|
| J | A | M | | L |
| | J | I | G | S |
| F | A | X | E | D |
| O | X | E | N | |
| X | | S | E | X |

## 43

| | | | | |
|---|---|---|---|---|
| C | H | A | L | K |
| R | A | V | E | N |
| A | B | A | T | E |
| S | L | I | M | E |
| S | A | L | E | S |

## 44

| | | | | |
|---|---|---|---|---|
| | S | L | A | P |
| S | C | I | F | I |
| P | U | T | I | N |
| E | B | E | R | T |
| D | A | R | E | |

## 45

| | | | | |
|---|---|---|---|---|
| | H | B | O | |
| B | O | O | B | Y |
| A | L | T | E | R |
| G | L | O | S | S |
| | A | X | E | |

## 46

| | | | | |
|---|---|---|---|---|
| D | E | A | T | H |
| E | | N | B | A |
| P | A | N | S | Y |
| O | N | E | | E |
| T | A | X | E | S |

## 47

| | | | | |
|---|---|---|---|---|
| | F | O | E | |
| B | R | U | S | H |
| R | I | N | S | E |
| O | S | C | A | R |
| | K | E | Y | |

## 48

| | | | | |
|---|---|---|---|---|
| H | I | N | D | I |
| O | N | I | O | N |
| S | L | O | B | S |
| T | A | B | L | E |
| S | W | E | E | T |

## 49

| | | | | |
|---|---|---|---|---|
| | A | P | P | S |
| T | W | E | R | K |
| H | A | N | O | I |
| A | R | A | B | S |
| I | D | L | E | |

## 50

| | | | | |
|---|---|---|---|---|
| | T | I | N | Y |
| A | I | M | | E |
| S | M | A | L | L |
| T | | C | A | P |
| I | T | S | Y | |

## 51

| | | | | |
|---|---|---|---|---|
| S | E | E | K | S |
| E | X | X | O | N |
| L | A | U | R | A |
| E | L | D | E | R |
| S | T | E | A | K |

## 52

| | | | | |
|---|---|---|---|---|
| A | F | T | E | R |
| D | O | W | ■ | O |
| D | R | E | A | M |
| U | ■ | E | R | A |
| P | U | T | I | N |

## 53

| | | | | |
|---|---|---|---|---|
| C | H | I | L | L |
| H | O | M | I | E |
| A | W | A | K | E |
| T | I | G | E | R |
| S | E | E | D | Y |

## 54

| | | | | |
|---|---|---|---|---|
| R | ■ | C | A | N |
| A | B | O | V | E |
| B | E | L | O | W |
| B | R | O | W | S |
| I | N | N | ■ | Y |

## 55

| | | | | |
|---|---|---|---|---|
| M | A | I | N | E |
| A | ■ | D | O | T |
| T | R | A | S | H |
| ■ | O | H | I | O |
| C | O | O | R | S |

## 56

| | | | | |
|---|---|---|---|---|
| J | E | S | S | E |
| I | T | A | ■ | L |
| M | C | R | I | B |
| M | ■ | A | D | O |
| Y | K | N | O | W |

## 57

| | | | | |
|---|---|---|---|---|
| C | U | P | ■ | V |
| O | B | A | M | A |
| L | E | G | A | L |
| D | R | A | K | E |
| S | ■ | N | E | T |

## 58

| | | | | |
|---|---|---|---|---|
| O | O | M | P | H |
| | H | E | R | A |
| H | A | D | E | S |
| A | R | E | S | |
| T | E | A | S | E |

## 59

| | | | | |
|---|---|---|---|---|
| S | W | I | P | E |
| H | | C | O | G |
| E | M | I | L | Y |
| E | O | N | | P |
| R | I | G | H | T |

## 60

| | | | | |
|---|---|---|---|---|
| S | A | P | P | Y |
| P | L | E | A | |
| F | L | A | I | L |
| | A | C | N | E |
| C | H | E | S | T |

## 61

| | | | | |
|---|---|---|---|---|
| | R | O | O | K |
| A | | M | R | I |
| Q | U | E | E | N |
| U | G | G | | G |
| A | H | A | B | |

## 62

| | | | | |
|---|---|---|---|---|
| S | C | A | R | P |
| P | I | X | A | R |
| A | L | I | T | O |
| R | I | O | T | S |
| K | A | N | Y | E |

## 63

| | | | | |
|---|---|---|---|---|
| M | Y | B | A | D |
| E | | R | O | W |
| E | B | O | L | A |
| T | O | W | | R |
| S | O | N | O | F |

## 64

| | | | | |
|---|---|---|---|---|
| | S | C | O | T |
| M | A | O | R | I |
| A | G | R | E | E |
| L | E | G | O | S |
| I | S | I | S | |

## 65

| | | | | |
|---|---|---|---|---|
| C | L | A | S | S |
| L | | L | I | T |
| O | Z | O | N | E |
| W | O | O | | R |
| N | O | F | U | N |

## 66

| | | | | |
|---|---|---|---|---|
| F | E | E | L | S |
| | | F | I | R |
| B | I | R | D | S |
| F | O | E | | |
| F | U | M | E | D |

**67**

| | | | | |
|---|---|---|---|---|
| | C | H | O | P |
| B | O | O | | O |
| I | N | U | S | E |
| D | | S | O | T |
| S | U | E | Y | |

**68**

| | | | | |
|---|---|---|---|---|
| J | O | C | K | |
| O | | H | I | C |
| B | L | I | T | Z |
| S | O | N | | A |
| | L | A | I | R |

**69**

| | | | | |
|---|---|---|---|---|
| J | E | T | E | R |
| O | | A | A | A |
| K | L | U | T | Z |
| E | O | N | | O |
| R | O | T | O | R |

## 70

| | | | | |
|---|---|---|---|---|
| G | I | A | N | T |
| A | R | M | | O |
| T | A | I | N | T |
| O | | T | E | A |
| R | O | Y | A | L |

## 71

| | | | | |
|---|---|---|---|---|
| R | A | D | A | R |
| | W | I | N | O |
| X | A | N | D | Y |
| X | K | E | S | |
| X | E | R | O | X |

## 72

| | | | | |
|---|---|---|---|---|
| C | A | N | D | Y |
| H | | E | V | E |
| O | H | A | R | A |
| N | U | T | | S |
| G | H | O | S | T |

**73**

| | | | | |
|---|---|---|---|---|
| | C | H | A | D |
| S | E | A | | I |
| H | O | U | S | E |
| I | | N | U | T |
| V | O | T | E | |

**74**

| | | | | |
|---|---|---|---|---|
| | A | D | D | |
| S | P | R | E | E |
| A | L | I | C | E |
| M | U | N | R | O |
| | S | K | Y | |

**75**

| | | | | |
|---|---|---|---|---|
| S | O | N | G | |
| C | U | O | M | O |
| A | T | B | A | R |
| N | O | L | I | E |
| | F | E | L | L |

## 76

| | | | | |
|---|---|---|---|---|
| A | D | V | I | L |
| L | E | O | ■ | A |
| B | E | L | L | Y |
| U | ■ | T | E | E |
| M | I | S | E | R |

## 77

| | | | | |
|---|---|---|---|---|
| P | R | O | ■ | O |
| R | E | C | U | T |
| M | I | T | C | H |
| A | D | E | L | E |
| N | ■ | T | A | R |

## 78

| | | | | |
|---|---|---|---|---|
| L | ■ | A | M | O |
| O | P | R | A | H |
| B | E | R | R | Y |
| B | R | O | K | E |
| Y | E | W | ■ | S |

## 79

| | | | | |
|---|---|---|---|---|
| T | I | M | E | S |
| W | | A | C | E |
| O | C | C | U | R |
| P | H | O | | B |
| M | I | N | U | S |

## 80

| | | | | |
|---|---|---|---|---|
| A | M | I | S | S |
| D | U | T | C | H |
| A | N | G | E | R |
| P | R | U | N | E |
| T | O | Y | E | D |

## 81

| | | | | |
|---|---|---|---|---|
| | Z | O | O | S |
| R | E | C | A | P |
| O | B | E | S | E |
| B | R | A | I | D |
| S | A | N | S | |

## 82

| | | | | |
|---|---|---|---|---|
| V | W | B | U | G |
| I | H | O | P | ■ |
| P | I | P | P | A |
| ■ | T | I | E | D |
| M | E | T | R | O |

## 83

| | | | | |
|---|---|---|---|---|
| S | W | I | N | G |
| N | O | N | ■ | R |
| A | E | T | N | A |
| K | ■ | H | A | S |
| E | V | E | N | S |

## 84

| | | | | |
|---|---|---|---|---|
| S | C | A | L | E |
| C | O | D | E | D |
| A | L | O | N | G |
| L | O | R | D | E |
| P | R | E | S | S |

## 85

| | | | | |
|---|---|---|---|---|
| G | O | N | Z | O |
| I | V | Y | | G |
| M | A | J | O | R |
| P | | E | W | E |
| Y | A | T | E | S |

## 86

| | | | | |
|---|---|---|---|---|
| D | | R | I | G |
| E | R | O | D | E |
| P | A | L | E | O |
| T | R | E | A | D |
| H | E | X | | E |

## 87

| | | | | |
|---|---|---|---|---|
| Z | E | R | O | G |
| | R | I | P | E |
| B | A | G | E | L |
| U | S | E | R | |
| D | E | L | A | Y |

**88**

| | | | | |
|---|---|---|---|---|
| | | E | C | G |
| | S | A | M | E |
| M | E | T | O | O |
| A | M | E | N | |
| W | I | N | | |

**89**

| | | | | |
|---|---|---|---|---|
| E | A | R | L | Y |
| G | R | A | Y | |
| G | O | B | I | G |
| | M | I | N | E |
| B | A | D | G | E |

**90**

| | | | | |
|---|---|---|---|---|
| S | P | A | M | |
| O | H | B | O | Y |
| T | O | N | T | O |
| S | T | E | E | L |
| | O | R | S | O |

## 91

| | | | | |
|---|---|---|---|---|
| C | | F | W | D |
| A | H | A | I | R |
| R | A | I | N | Y |
| T | I | L | D | E |
| E | L | S | | R |

## 92

| | | | | |
|---|---|---|---|---|
| A | C | R | I | D |
| R | I | O | | E |
| E | A | G | E | R |
| N | | U | S | E |
| A | L | E | C | K |

## 93

| | | | | |
|---|---|---|---|---|
| C | A | L | L | |
| A | L | O | O | F |
| R | I | D | G | E |
| L | E | G | O | S |
| | N | E | S | T |

## 94

| | | | | |
|---|---|---|---|---|
| C | H | E | C | K |
| H | E | M | A | N |
| I | N | A | N | E |
| P | R | I | D | E |
| S | I | L | O | S |

## 95

| | | | | |
|---|---|---|---|---|
| D | I | T | Z | Y |
| E | ■ | R | E | I |
| P | L | A | N | E |
| T | A | I | ■ | L |
| H | O | N | E | D |

## 96

| | | | | |
|---|---|---|---|---|
| ■ | F | A | L | L |
| B | L | T | ■ | I |
| O | U | T | D | O |
| O | ■ | I | A | N |
| M | A | C | Y | S |

## 97

| | | | | |
|---|---|---|---|---|
| | S | K | I | |
| H | A | N | N | A |
| A | L | A | D | Y |
| L | E | V | I | N |
| | S | E | A | |

## 98

| | | | | |
|---|---|---|---|---|
| | K | U | R | D |
| J | O | N | | E |
| P | I | Z | Z | A |
| E | | I | O | N |
| G | A | P | E | |

## 99

| | | | | |
|---|---|---|---|---|
| J | | R | O | W |
| E | V | E | N | |
| W | O | M | E | N |
| | L | I | K | E |
| S | E | X | | W |

## 100

| | | | | |
|---|---|---|---|---|
| | C | A | V | S |
| P | U | P | I | L |
| O | B | A | M | A |
| C | A | R | E | Y |
| O | N | T | O | |

## 101

| | | | | |
|---|---|---|---|---|
| P | | S | I | X |
| A | C | I | D | |
| W | A | T | E | R |
| | B | A | S | E |
| F | O | R | | D |

## 102

| | | | | |
|---|---|---|---|---|
| F | T | L | E | E |
| O | W | E | N | S |
| R | E | A | D | S |
| G | E | N | O | A |
| E | N | T | R | Y |

## 103

| | | | | |
|---|---|---|---|---|
| T | A | M | P | A |
| W | I | I | ■ | W |
| O | M | A | H | A |
| L | ■ | M | A | R |
| B | O | I | S | E |

## 104

| | | | | |
|---|---|---|---|---|
| R | A | B | B | I |
| ■ | G | A | L | L |
| H | A | G | E | L |
| U | V | E | A | ■ |
| B | E | L | T | S |

## 105

| | | | | |
|---|---|---|---|---|
| ■ | C | H | O | ■ |
| C | R | A | S | H |
| G | E | I | C | O |
| I | D | T | A | G |
| ■ | S | I | R | ■ |

## 106

| | | | | |
|---|---|---|---|---|
| A | C | T | | M |
| | L | I | S | A |
| H | O | M | E | R |
| A | G | I | N | G |
| T | | D | D | E |

## 107

| | | | | |
|---|---|---|---|---|
| A | E | S | O | P |
| | M | E | M | O |
| W | I | R | E | D |
| P | L | U | G | |
| M | Y | M | A | N |

## 108

| | | | | |
|---|---|---|---|---|
| | M | E | M | E |
| L | O | X | E | S |
| E | X | E | R | T |
| W | I | C | C | A |
| D | E | S | K | |

## 109

| | | | | |
|---|---|---|---|---|
| | B | A | M | |
| J | O | L | I | E |
| A | G | I | N | G |
| R | U | B | I | O |
| | S | I | S | |

## 110

| | | | | |
|---|---|---|---|---|
| | C | A | S | K |
| C | A | R | L | A |
| L | I | M | I | T |
| I | R | O | N | Y |
| P | O | R | K | |

## 111

| | | | | |
|---|---|---|---|---|
| B | O | M | B | S |
| | P | O | O | L |
| K | E | R | R | Y |
| I | R | A | N | |
| M | A | L | E | S |

## 112

| | | | | |
|---|---|---|---|---|
| | B | I | A | S |
| S | O | A | M | I |
| C | O | M | I | C |
| U | Z | B | E | K |
| M | E | S | S | |

## 113

| | | | | |
|---|---|---|---|---|
| | B | A | D | |
| B | A | C | O | N |
| I | S | U | Z | U |
| B | E | R | E | T |
| | D | A | N | |

## 114

| | | | | |
|---|---|---|---|---|
| H | A | P | P | Y |
| | S | U | R | E |
| C | H | R | I | S |
| H | E | R | D | |
| E | S | S | E | X |

## 115

| | | | | |
|---|---|---|---|---|
| C | U | T | I | E |
| Y | ■ | R | O | M |
| C | H | A | S | M |
| L | E | D | ■ | Y |
| E | X | E | C | S |

## 116

| | | | | |
|---|---|---|---|---|
| ■ | A | B | A | R |
| S | T | I | L | E |
| N | O | L | I | E |
| I | N | B | E | D |
| P | E | O | N | ■ |

## 117

| | | | | |
|---|---|---|---|---|
| ■ | W | I | L | Y |
| D | I | X | I | E |
| A | P | N | E | A |
| M | E | A | N | S |
| E | D | Y | S | ■ |

## 118

| | | | | |
|---|---|---|---|---|
| J | A | R | | P |
| E | V | O | K | E |
| R | O | B | I | N |
| K | N | O | W | N |
| Y | | T | I | E |

## 119

| | | | | |
|---|---|---|---|---|
| L | A | T | K | E |
| A | W | W | | V |
| R | E | A | D | E |
| G | | N | U | N |
| E | I | G | H | T |

## 120

| | | | | |
|---|---|---|---|---|
| | S | U | P | |
| M | A | N | O | R |
| A | U | D | I | O |
| O | N | E | N | D |
| | A | R | T | |

## 121

| | | | | |
|---|---|---|---|---|
| A | B | S | | L |
| | O | T | T | O |
| S | N | E | R | T |
| O | D | I | E | |
| Y | | N | E | W |

## 122

| | | | | |
|---|---|---|---|---|
| C | A | R | G | O |
| A | L | A | R | M |
| R | O | G | U | E |
| T | H | O | N | G |
| S | A | N | T | A |

## 123

| | | | | |
|---|---|---|---|---|
| | V | H | S | |
| B | E | I | N | G |
| I | N | K | E | Y |
| B | T | E | A | M |
| | I | R | K | |

## 124

| | | | | |
|---|---|---|---|---|
| O | A | T | H | ■ |
| P | ■ | H | I | S |
| E | J | E | C | T |
| D | U | O | ■ | E |
| ■ | S | C | A | M |

## 125

| | | | | |
|---|---|---|---|---|
| C | H | I | R | P |
| R | E | F | E | R |
| E | N | N | U | I |
| S | C | O | N | E |
| T | E | T | E | S |

## 126

| | | | | |
|---|---|---|---|---|
| G | M | C | ■ | G |
| E | U | L | E | R |
| C | L | A | R | A |
| K | L | U | T | Z |
| O | ■ | S | E | E |

## 127

| | | | | |
|---|---|---|---|---|
| | S | A | C | |
| P | A | U | L | A |
| O | N | T | A | P |
| S | T | O | U | T |
| | A | S | S | |

## 128

| | | | | |
|---|---|---|---|---|
| O | | H | O | P |
| S | H | A | V | E |
| C | O | M | E | T |
| A | P | A | R | T |
| R | E | S | | Y |

## 129

| | | | | |
|---|---|---|---|---|
| S | L | A | M | |
| O | | W | O | K |
| D | U | M | B | O |
| A | S | A | | C |
| | A | N | K | H |

**130**

| | | | | |
|---|---|---|---|---|
| | C | U | B | A |
| F | I | D | E | L |
| D | R | D | R | E |
| I | C | E | R | S |
| C | A | R | Y | |

**131**

| | | | | |
|---|---|---|---|---|
| M | M | X | V | |
| U | | R | I | B |
| S | P | A | D | E |
| T | O | Y | | A |
| | E | S | P | N |

**132**

| | | | | |
|---|---|---|---|---|
| C | H | U | C | K |
| R | O | S | E | |
| Y | O | U | N | G |
| | H | A | T | E |
| F | A | L | S | E |

## 133

| | | | | |
|---|---|---|---|---|
| A | U | L | D | |
| N | | O | R | B |
| T | A | H | O | E |
| | L | A | N | G |
| S | Y | N | E | |

## 134

| | | | | |
|---|---|---|---|---|
| L | A | S | S | O |
| A | I | L | | N |
| T | R | I | B | E |
| E | | C | O | P |
| R | A | K | I | M |

## 135

| | | | | |
|---|---|---|---|---|
| O | | S | P | Y |
| M | A | T | E | |
| G | U | E | S | S |
| | R | A | T | E |
| R | A | M | | W |

**136**

| | | | | |
|---|---|---|---|---|
| M | Y | T | H | ■ |
| A | ■ | H | U | G |
| P | H | O | T | O |
| S | I | R | ■ | N |
| ■ | S | N | U | G |

**137**

| | | | | |
|---|---|---|---|---|
| N | O | D | U | H |
| O | V | E | N | ■ |
| M | A | N | I | C |
| ■ | R | I | O | T |
| H | Y | M | N | S |

**138**

| | | | | |
|---|---|---|---|---|
| ■ | A | S | S | ■ |
| B | L | U | E | S |
| O | L | I | V | E |
| K | O | T | E | X |
| ■ | Y | E | N | ■ |

## 139

| | | | | |
|---|---|---|---|---|
| W | O | R | D | ■ |
| A | H | E | A | D |
| S | H | I | N | E |
| P | E | N | C | E |
| ■ | Y | S | E | R |

## 140

| | | | | |
|---|---|---|---|---|
| ■ | B | R | I | E |
| A | R | E | ■ | D |
| G | O | U | D | A |
| U | ■ | S | U | M |
| A | G | E | D | ■ |

## 141

| | | | | |
|---|---|---|---|---|
| A | S | H | ■ | A |
| ■ | H | A | M | M |
| D | O | P | E | Y |
| O | O | P | S | ■ |
| C | ■ | Y | A | Y |

## 142

| | | | | |
|---|---|---|---|---|
| P | L | A | Y | |
| O | | S | I | P |
| R | H | I | N | O |
| K | I | D | | S |
| | T | E | X | T |

## 143

| | | | | |
|---|---|---|---|---|
| S | L | E | D | S |
| L | E | V | E | L |
| A | G | I | L | E |
| B | I | T | T | E |
| S | T | E | A | K |

## 144

| | | | | |
|---|---|---|---|---|
| | K | I | M | |
| R | E | V | E | L |
| E | N | O | L | A |
| P | Y | R | E | X |
| | A | Y | E | |

## 145

| | | | | |
|---|---|---|---|---|
| | A | W | E | D |
| B | R | A | V | E |
| L | E | V | I | S |
| V | N | E | C | K |
| D | A | R | T | |

## 146

| | | | | |
|---|---|---|---|---|
| | P | A | D | |
| M | L | K | J | R |
| P | U | R | S | E |
| G | O | O | E | Y |
| | T | N | T | |

## 147

| | | | | |
|---|---|---|---|---|
| D | I | S | C | S |
| U | H | A | U | L |
| V | E | N | M | O |
| E | A | T | I | T |
| T | R | A | N | S |

## 148

| | | | | |
|---|---|---|---|---|
| ■ | H | U | L | U |
| H | Y | P | E | R |
| I | D | T | A | G |
| G | R | O | P | E |
| H | A | N | S | ■ |

## 149

| | | | | |
|---|---|---|---|---|
| S | N | O | W | S |
| A | N | N | I | E |
| S | W | E | L | L |
| S | ■ | A | D | M |
| Y | U | M | ■ | A |

## 150

| | | | | |
|---|---|---|---|---|
| M | O | S | E | S |
| A | ■ | C | ■ | C |
| G | R | A | P | E |
| M | E | L | O | N |
| A | P | P | L | E |

# Looking for more Hard Crosswords?

## The New York Times

The #1 Name in Crosswords

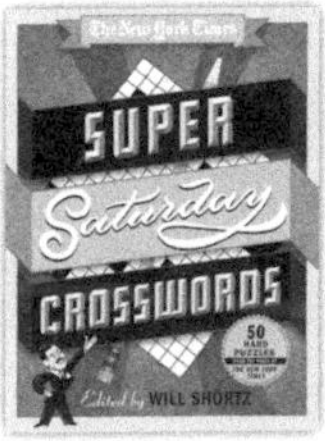

Available at your local bookstore or online at nytimes.com/store/books

St. Martin's Griffin

## Looking for more Large-Print Crosswords?

# The New York Times

The #1 Name in Crosswords

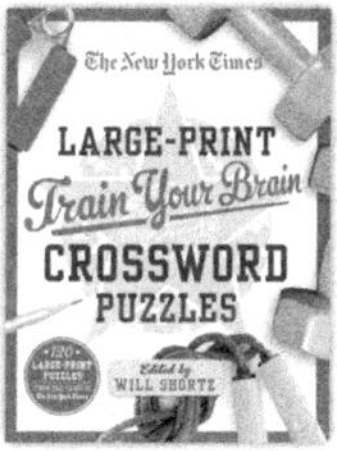

Looking for more Sunday Crosswords?

# The New York Times

The #1 Name in Crosswords

Available at your local bookstore or online at nytimes.com/store/books

St. Martin's Griffin